Evangelical Christians find them  toward their beliefs, and the Bib sexuality are especially under attack. And when Christians stand up for their beliefs, they are called hateful, bigoted, and antiquated. Many believers have grown weary in the fight and wonder if they should withdraw from the controversy or simply concede. In the midst of the current crisis, *Dangerous Affirmation* powerfully and succinctly addresses key issues, including how we got here in our society, making sense of pro-LGBT readings of the scriptures and why they ultimately fail, and asking if the Bible's teaching on sexuality is still relevant in a modern society. M.D. Perkins reminds us that God is the creator, and it is He who knows what is best for His creation. As you read this book, you'll be reminded that our society needs the transforming power of the Gospel now as much as ever.

**Dr. Michael L. Brown,** Host, *The Line of Fire* radio broadcast; Author, *Can You Be Gay and Christian?*

In *Dangerous Affirmation*, M.D. Perkins details the wonder and beauty of God's created intent for human sexuality. However, he also confronts the reality of the Fall, which disordered and distorted God's order for human beings. In a clear, convincing, and compassionate manner, M.D. Perkins magnifies God's purpose for human sexuality, detailing that God created male and female as complementary beings and that the privilege of sexual expression between a man and woman is honored in the context of covenant marriage. Consequently, both heterosexual and homosexual sexual behavior outside of the covenant of marriage violates God's intention and distorts the human spirit. Perkins, in a pastoral manner, highlights the issues that disorder God's purpose and then points to the power of the gospel of Jesus Christ as the only means to transform lives ravaged by sin. The hopeful result is a new creation that turns our hearts to a renewed purpose: to be conformed to the likeness of Christ alone.

**Dr. Dominic Aquila,** President, New Geneva Theological Seminary

Few movements threaten the Gospel of Jesus Christ more than the radical homosexual movement. Any thinking, studious, Spirit-led Jesus-follower knows that the Bible does not affirm homosexual activity. But many so-called "Christians" have muddled thinking on this issue. *Dangerous Affirmation* will clean out the muddled thinking and replace it with biblical and factual reality. Buy a book. Read it. In fact, buy several books and give them to people who need to be introduced or reintroduced to authentic biblical Christianity on this issue.

**Dr. Jim Garlow**, CEO, Well Versed

The LGBT movement has been pushing into the church for decades, and it is past time that Christians wake up to the deception. *Dangerous Affirmation* is one of the most important books of our time. It shows us how we got here and what we can do to stand firm. If Christians are going to spread the light of Jesus, we cannot affirm lies. We must speak the truth in love. This book helps us to do that.

**Dr. Robert Jeffress**, Senior Pastor, First Baptist Church, Dallas, Texas

M.D. Perkins has put forth the most thorough evidence for what we are seeing take place in the world today with the inclusion and acceptance of errant sexuality in the church. Perkins tackles with great decorum and intentionality the difficult but necessary topic of the broken ideology of progressive Christianity and the embrace of all things LGBTQ+ that are destroying the church from within. Alongside Dr. Robert Gagnon, this is the best work I've seen on the topic—uncovering the difficult truth about "gay Christianity" and "sexual minorities." Every church needs this book. Every Bible-believing Christian needs this book. It's factual, it's easy to read, and it's full of everything one needs to know in order to interpret correctly what is happening in America today. As a men's minister who has himself come out of homosexuality, I believe this book nails it.

**Jim Farrington**, Men's Minister, First Stone Ministries, Oklahoma City, Oklahoma

The Bible is not silent about sexuality and homosexuality. Yet the biblical teaching on sex, sexual attraction, and marriage is under attack by those within the church. This makes the threat to the church all the more dangerous. This is why I am thankful for *Dangerous Affirmation*. M.D. Perkins has written the book that needed to be written. It is a gracious but uncompromising rebuttal to the various arguments affirming "gay Christianity" and same-sex attraction. This is an excellent resource for pastors and counselors as it functions as a comprehensive handbook on the topic. This is also an excellent resource for Christian parents who have children struggling with same-sex attraction and for all those who sincerely desire to know what God thinks about sexuality.

**Jeffrey D. Johnson**, President, Grace Bible Theological Seminary; Pastor, Grace Bible Church, Conway, Arkansas

*Dangerous Affirmation* is a thoroughly researched and well-written balance of truth and love. I believe it is one of the most important works about one of the gravest threats to the church and the world in a millennium. M.D. Perkins has taken up the gospel sword and charged head on into the battle—raising the banner of Christ and providing a tool for the church to answer the sexual revolution's efforts to subtly infiltrate Christ's bride through shrewd deception.

**Les Riley**, President, Personhood Alliance

This is a wonderful sourcebook that every Christian needs. If you want to read a book that will quickly give you a clear picture of the LGBTQ movement alongside clear biblical analysis, you are holding it in your hand. In *Dangerous Affirmation*, M.D. Perkins has given us a thoroughly biblical analysis of the current attacks against Christian morality through the LGBTQ movement. He simply and carefully dissects the various nuances of the spectrums of personalities and ideas in the clearest way, and he provides the biblical truth to help you understand how to think about them. I highly recommend it.

**Scott T. Brown**, President, Church and Family Life; Pastor, Hope Baptist Church, Wake Forest, North Carolina

M.D. Perkins has been watching the sexuality battle rage across the Western world. What really concerned him, though, was the church's growing vulnerability to the enemies' lies. It is from love for God's people that he wrote *Dangerous Affirmation: The Threat of "Gay Christianity."* Perkins did his homework. He spent a lot of time studying the lies, yet he didn't allow his study and writing to drag him down into anger and culture wars. His heart and tone are pastoral—not meaning weak, but protective and loving. The documentation is excellent. If you're a father of the church calling sinners to repentance and defending God's sheep, you'll find Perkins's work an excellent help.

**Tim Bayly**, Pastor, Trinity Reformed Church, Bloomington, Indiana; Coauthor, *The Grace of Shame: 7 Ways the Church Has Failed to Love Homosexuals*

One of the greatest challenges facing the Christian church in the twenty-first century is the nature of reality itself. Progressive activists from academia to the medical community to the halls of political power loudly and repeatedly tell us that that many of the long-accepted categories that have informed our understanding of nature—including human nature—are mere social constructs. Objective standards by which to distinguish between maleness and femaleness are scoffed at as oppressive and harmful. Self-determination, including the determination of one's own sexual identity, is the new ethic; and affirming such determinations is now one of the greatest virtues.

Nowhere is this revolt against God's created order made more manifest than in the "gay Christian" movement. The very concept is an overthrow of the transformative nature of biblical Christianity. But failure to recognize and even affirm "gay Christians" is to violate the new norms and make oneself a target of those who demand affirmation. Consequently, a growing number of Christians have been led into affirming that which God does not recognize as real—"gay Christians."

M.D. Perkins recognizes this trap and helps Christians avoid falling into it by evaluating the "gay Christian" movement in the light of scripture. He demonstrates both its metaphysical impossibility as well as its moral irrationality as he highlights and contends for an ethic that is grounded solidly in the Bible's teaching on sexuality. Carefully researched, thoughtfully argued, and sensitively presented, this book will help Christians see clearly where the problems are in many of the ways that believers have engaged this issue and, more importantly, where the proper pathways are for a more loving and redemptive engagement.

**Tom Ascol**, President, Founders Ministries

The soul of the evangelical church hangs in the balance: will she or will she not transform her views of personhood, anthropology, ethics, and exegesis to be more acceptable to modern sexual culture? M.D. Perkins both informs and calls the Body of Christ to not be fooled or bullied. His excellent work provides copious and careful definitions and historical background on key concepts such as homosexuality, affirming theology, queer theology, gay celibate theology, aesthetic orientation, spiritual friendship, and more. He shines a light on fake biblical exegesis, which more serves the heart of fallen culture than the heart of God. He even dares to highlight the apologetic strategies employed inside and outside the church by those who prefer to blame the Lord's people rather than call them to more careful devotion to their Head and Husband. The American Family Association is to be commended for this fine work. What will be left of the American family if the evangelical church fails to speak the truth in love to such tragic error?

**Dr. W. Duncan Rankin**, Professor of Systematic Theology, Blue Ridge Institute for Theological Education

Having spent significant time with the author, I have seen up close a young Joshua burdened by God to write on a topic that few dare approach. M.D.'s sensitive, truth-telling presentation in the Christ-centered book you hold in your hand is the work of a sober-minded Christian scholar. In *Dangerous Affirmation*, I believe God has called M.D. to present the heart and mind of God on "gay Christianity" so that those who are embattled and weary are not numbered with those who cower back and are foolish but as those who understand the times and know how to live and—if need be—die in Him.

**Bill Johnson**, President, American Decency Association

There was a time when evangelicals were essentially unified in viewing homosexuality as an abomination. However, with groups like Revoice advancing the concept of "gay Christianity" and Living Out normalizing the idea of "same-sex attraction," confusion abounds even among many conservative Christians. The voices causing confusion come from multiple directions. On the one hand, Christians are bombarded by progressive voices of the world who are working to alter the culture's and church's attitudes towards homosexuality. On the other hand, leading evangelical voices are saying that "God whispers" about homosexual sin.

In these confusing times, I am thankful for the voice of M.D. Perkins, who speaks with biblical clarity. He will help the reader understand the unbiblical theology of the "gay Christian" movement and reveals the "endgame" that seeks "to create LGBT activists and allies within the walls of the Christian church." Every Christian needs to have a sound biblical worldview on homosexuality and confidence that the gospel is powerful to transform those who are entrapped in the LGBT lifestyle. This is exactly what *Dangerous Affirmation* provides.

**Tom Buck**, Senior Pastor, First Baptist Church, Lindale, Texas

Those who endorse homosexual behavior as acceptable within Christian norms find it necessary to justify their view by developing exegetical arguments dealing with biblical texts that are traditionally interpreted as prohibiting same-sex practice. This book presents a devastating rebuttal to such revisionist theology, exposing the fallacy of its logic by addressing texts pertaining to the issue with sound hermeneutical principles. Perkins's treatment of the subject is totally devoid of any lame proof-texting, as he discusses each passage within its proper context and setting. The result is a nonpartisan assessment of the biblical material that avoids both homophilic and homophobic presuppositions. Those who are committed to the Bible as God's authoritative word will find strong affirmation in this book, and those who have denied that divine authority by their endorsement of same-gender relationships will find this book to be a strong challenge to their position.

**Dr. Jerry Horner**, Founding Dean, Regent University School of Divinity

*Dangerous Affirmation* is well-titled. It's a crystal-clear exposition of scriptural truth that refutes the many myths, false "science," dangerous claims, and outright lies of so-called "gay Christianity." This readable, well-documented book takes on the wolves among the sheep who have seduced so many in the church into moral relativism and theological error under the guise of misguided "compassion."

**Robert Knight**, Author of *The Age of Consent: The Rise of Relativism and the Corruption of Popular Culture*; Columnist

The rider on the white horse in Revelation 19 is called "Faithful and True." His followers yearn to be known by those virtues. Yet we live in a world that is the antithesis of those words. One of the issues that seeks to undermine our quest to be faithful and true is unbiblical sexuality. Most believers know what the Bible says about homosexuality. The secular response to it is expected. But the voices within the church calling for accommodating homosexuality promote great confusion among the faithful. M.D. Perkins has provided a remarkable tool for those who desire to remain faithful and true to their Savior. Every assertion that erodes biblical confidence is more than adequately addressed in this book. Any reasonable person will know after finishing this book that there is no such thing as "Gay Christianity."

**Dr. Raymond Rooney, Jr.**, Digital Editor, The Stand

Modern man has come along and decided to rewrite the dictionary on the subject of marriage, family, and human sexuality. Just a simple stroll through the bookstore will tell you that we have a true fascination with the subject of human sexuality. Unfortunately, the majority of the books are written from a lens of modern psychology, taking their root in the dictionary of man rather than the dictionary of God. In order to rethink the boundaries of human sexuality, you must first rethink God. In this excellent book, M.D. Perkins deals with the root and the fruit of the modern progressive movement regarding human sexuality through the lens of scripture.

**Dr. Josh Buice**, Pastor, Pray's Mill Baptist Church, Douglasville, Georgia; Founder and President, G3 Ministries

M.D. Perkins has written the definitive exposé of the "Gay Christianity" movement. The time has come to draw a line in the sand. You can support "gay rights," or you can stand on the Word of God. There is no middle ground. Here's my suggestion: buy two copies—one to read and one to give to your pastor. It's that good!

**Dr. Ray Pritchard**, President, Keep Believing Ministries; AFA Board Member

In *Dangerous Affirmation*, M.D. Perkins has greatly benefitted the church with his clear, powerful, and scholarly defense of traditional biblical sexual ethics. He has laid bare the subterfuge and folly of modern teachings that seek to distort and corrupt the Word of God to the end that license be given to immorality and abomination. This book is a breath of fresh air in the midst of the stifling moral relativism and sexual confusion of our day and will certainly take its place as a foundational apologetic "for the faith which was once for all delivered to the saints" (Jude 1:3b). I rejoice that God has raised up articulate thinkers and communicators like M.D. Perkins, and I heartily support and commend his excellent work.

**Daniel T. Gilmore**, District Superintendent, Church of the Nazarene

M.D. Perkins brings clarity to the LGBT movement that is responsible for infiltrating and saturating our schools, churches, and families with gay theology. The Bible warns of the times we are living in, yet sadly many have not paid attention or dared to stand against the LGBT movement and the destruction it causes. M.D. demonstrates great courage in writing *Dangerous Affirmation* from a heart that desires to address "gay Christianity" with truth and compassion from God's Word. May each reader come to a better understanding of where we are and how we got here.

**Denise Shick**, Founder and Executive Director, Help 4 Families Ministries

In this book. M.D. Perkins sounds a clarion call for the church to be the church.

Although he does not say it in so many words, he shows that the phrase "gay Christianity" is an oxymoron. Carefully, and with measured language, he examines the claims of "gay Christians" in the light of the biblical instructions and shows how the two are incompatible. At the heart of his argument is the claim that homosexual desire is not an "orientation" to be accepted but a temptation to be overcome. This is a book that will equip thoughtful believers to address the challenge of homosexuality and the church with clarity.

**John N. Oswalt, Ph.D.**, Visiting Distinguished Professor of Old Testament, Asbury Theological Seminary

This powerful volume by M.D. Perkins is another of God's wake-up calls to an American church adrift and in much need of realignment in these essential matters of sexuality, identity, biblical interpretation and Christian living. He pulls back the curtain on an unbiblical affirmation of the LGBTQ agenda infecting the body of Christ. He gives the reader in particular and the church in general a concise, clear, compassionate and well-documented diagnosis along with the ultimate cure in Christ and biblical fidelity. Perkins challenges every local church to do some soul-searching and to face with courage and compassion the "dangerous affirmation" of a false gospel veiled in the language of "love" and "truth" that now permeates many churches and denominations. This book will move pastors and laity alike to carefully consider any capitulation in its ranks and to recommit to God's gracious and good plan for humanity's redemption and restoration.

"Though they know God's decree that those who practice such things deserve to die, they not only do them but give approval to those who practice them." — Romans 1:32

**Dr. Jeff Switzer**, Pastor, Trinity United Methodist Church, Gulfport, Mississippi; AFA Board Chairman

With careful analysis, copious research, and biblical fealty, M.D. Perkins and the American Family Association have done a great service in exposing the threat that "gay" Christianity poses not only to the health of the church but to culture and society in general. Mr. Perkins meticulously unpacks the nuances of the terminology and arguments that attempt to put a righteous face on a toxic worldview. Though the public discourse around us might sometimes wax hateful, Mr. Perkins is guided by a deep love for his fellow Christian, his fellow American, and his fellow man. This is a much-needed book one would do well to read.

**Richard G. Howe, Ph.D.**, Provost and Professor of Philosophy and Apologetics, Norman L. Geisler Chair of Christian Apologetics, Southern Evangelical Seminary

*Dangerous Affirmation* is clear, comprehensive, and biblically sound. We are deeply indebted to M.D. Perkins for exposing the theological, biblical, ecclesiastical, and social implications of "gay Christianity" and for calling us to biblical faithfulness. I cannot recommend this book too highly.

**Gareth Lee Cockerill**, Professor Emeritus of New Testament and Biblical Theology, Wesley Biblical Seminary

# DANGEROUS AFFIRMATION

## The Threat of "Gay Christianity"

# M.D. PERKINS

American Family Association
Tupelo, Mississippi

American Family Association
107 Parkgate Drive
Tupelo, Mississippi 38801
www.afa.net

Printed in the United States of America
Signature Book Printing, www.sbpbooks.com

ISBN 978-1-935932-37-6

Cover design by Canada Burns

Editorial contributions by Randall Murphree, Rebecca Davis, and Ed Vitagliano

*Dedicated to my dear brother in the faith,*
*David H. Linden,*
*who, at 79 years old, taught me that*
*life is too short and Christ is too precious*
*to remain silent when His church is under attack.*

*Make no mistake. We as Bible-believing evangelical Christians are locked in a battle. This is not a friendly gentleman's discussion. It is a life and death conflict between the spiritual hosts of wickedness and those who claim the name of Christ. It is a conflict on the level of ideas between two fundamentally opposed views of truth and reality. It is a conflict on the level of actions between a complete moral perversion and chaos and God's absolutes.*

*But do we really believe that we are in a life and death battle?*

— Francis Schaeffer, *The Great Evangelical Disaster*

# TABLE OF CONTENTS

# FOREWORD **BY STEPHEN H. BLACK**

*You can't go back and change the beginning, but you can start where you are and change the ending.* — C.S. Lewis

*Those who do not learn from history are doomed to repeat it.* — George Santayana

*Dangerous Affirmation* **is needed more today than ever before in history as the "gay Christian" movement poses a real threat to the church of Jesus Christ.** Unfortunately, it seems we have not learned from the sexual revolution of the 1960s concerning the destruction of sexual sin. Although we cannot go back and change what has transpired, we can continue to preach the truth and work diligently to see a different ending—no matter how dark or dishonest our times may seem. Because of our failure to learn from our own mistakes, the church in America finds herself in a dark time. Nevertheless, we trust there is a day of transformation coming, as the Word of God promises.

The culture around us is sex-saturated, yet those living by their sexual appetites are unfulfilled, still longing for real love. This is true for many in so-called "affirming congregations" as well—they may have affirmation, yet they lack true Christian love. The church is filled with compromise on the issues of unnatural desires, and *Dangerous Affirmation* is a clarion call to a much-needed return to biblical orthodoxy. There is power, wisdom, and common sense in God's Word—a place where we can all experience the real love of God.

There are many Christian leaders and evangelicals who have capitulated by embracing poor theology, distorted sociology, and forgetful anthropology. These men and women leaders seem happy to embrace all things LGBT as long as they call themselves "Christian." There are those who would have us rethink or revoice the Bible according to the whims of our current culture. M.D. Perkins has exposed these dangerous affirmations of leaven. For we know that "a little leaven leavens the whole lump" (Galatians 5:9). Or, as the New Living Translation (NLT) renders it, "These false teachings are like a little yeast that spreads through the whole batch of dough!"

The Bible clearly warns of the days in which we are living. It warns that many would be scoffers and mockers in teaching doctrines of impurity that turn the grace of God into acceptable lewdness in word, thought, and deed (2 Timothy 3:1–7, 2 Peter 2:1–22, 2 Peter 3:1–7). It is the American Psychological Association's "orientation gospel" that is promoted— both knowingly and unknowingly—in some of the highest places in Christianity: seminaries, Christian colleges, and churches big and small. As we write, there are those who are calling "sexual minorities" a legitimate Christian group and moving others to accept LGBT desires and behaviors in the church. These ideas are introduced through the acceptance of unbiblical, psychological word-groupings: "Gay Christian." "Queer Christian." "Same-sex attracted Christian." This book is a clear declaration to resist systemic unbelief throughout the body of Christ and a call for Christian leaders to contend earnestly for the saving faith of our Lord Jesus Christ (Jude 1:3–7).

M.D. Perkins gives us an exhortation to embrace Jesus' message of transformative grace. He calls for us to leave behind the lies of the "orientation" narrative and the so-called "grace" that leaves souls stuck in their unnatural affections—leading to the further bondage of unbelief. He is rightfully holding up the standard of biblically orthodox truth that is the very message of the cross of Christ. This holy truth has the power to deliver those who truly love the Light and submit to Jesus Christ as Lord (2 Corinthians 4:1–6). Jesus was clear in His gospel that a saving faith will produce repentance and results in believing for an entire life of righteousness (Matthew 7:13–28, Romans 10:8–13). *Dangerous Affirmation* gives a grace-filled offering of biblical truth and of great hope for those who will believe the truth found in these pages.

Many influential Christian leaders—believing themselves to be wise and compassionate—promote the American Psychological Association's view of "orientation" as right and true. They insert this claim into their affirming theology. *Dangerous Affirmation: The Threat of "Gay Christianity"* confronts this deception head on. M.D. Perkins points us back to the authority of the Word of God as the standard by which we are to measure our behaviors, feelings, thoughts, and even our so-called "orientations." He also does an excellent job of unpacking gay celibate theology, which promotes a distorted identity through normalizing unnatural affections. *Dangerous Affirmation* is written clearly and without compromise. Many theologians today would benefit from reading this clear, concise offering of love. It is a short read that is power-packed and should be shared with every pastor and Christian leader you know.

On a personal note, M.D. Perkins is a kind and gentle man who did not wake up one day desiring a battle with those who are gay-identified. He is a man who has seen the battle for truth and scriptural clarity coming to his own church and has lovingly responded in grace. I am a man who left homosexuality behind over 38 years ago. This is important because I have never witnessed this author to be unkind or unloving as a way of life toward anyone—especially someone who is living in or has lived through sexual distortion.

We are all indebted for this contribution of grace and love. I am proud to work with the American Family Association (and their American Family Studios film project *In His Image: Delighting in God's Plan for Gender and Sexuality*) in bringing bold truth with bold love. I am also blessed to call M.D. Perkins a friend.

Stephen H. Black<br>
Pastor, Speaker, Author

# INTRODUCTION

# WHAT IS "GAY CHRISTIANITY"?

In October of 1968, a group of people met for worship in a living room in the Huntington Park neighborhood of Los Angeles. The group was small—twelve people in total—led by a dynamic young preacher named Troy Perry. A former Pentecostal preacher from north Florida who had recently come out of the closet as a homosexual, Perry was nervous about the gathering, but he was emboldened by an epiphany that he believed came from God: a vision to create an affirming church for the gay community.

Out of this meeting, the Metropolitan Community Church (MCC) was born—the first Protestant denomination to openly affirm and celebrate homosexuality and to actively work for lesbian, gay, bisexual, and transgender (LGBT) social causes worldwide. Today, Metropolitan Community Church continues to present its vision of theological liberalism and progressive LGBT activism in communities across the country. But the most influential legacy of Troy Perry is not in himself or MCC churches but in kindling a broader movement to affirm homosexuality within the Christian church. This movement is what we know as "gay Christianity."

Throughout two thousand years of church history, Christians have understood—and Christian churches have taught—that homosexuality is a sin. It is "against nature" (Romans 1:26–27). It is an "abomination" (Leviticus 18:22, 20:13). It can be described as "vile affections" or "dishonorable passions" (Romans 1:26). It is not God's design for marriage or family (Genesis 2:18–25). It is something that God does not bless, nor can He because it is defiantly against His revealed will (1 Corinthians 6:9–10). And because it is against God's will and design, to embrace and celebrate homosexuality is to evoke God's judgment—as an individual, church, or nation (Genesis 19:1–29). Since Christianity first took root in the West, the Bible's teaching against homosexuality has defined public policy and social attitudes in Europe and America.

But things have changed.

Since the 1960s, a growing number of professing Christians have been arguing against the biblical facts. It has been said that the Bible's teaching of love should be celebrated while the Bible's sexual ethics should be rethought or rejected. It has been said that orthodox theology is oppressive and harmful while affirming theology is life-giving and beautiful. It has been said that a person who identifies as a "gay Christian" is simply part of God's plan for a diverse church. It has been said that being gay is innate and immutable and that anyone who claims that a gay person can change is a liar. It has been said that in order to truly love our neighbors, Christians must fight for LGBT causes in the political arena. These are all expressions of "gay Christianity."

Fundamentally, *gay Christianity* is the attempt to

reconcile the Christian faith with homosexuality. I use "gay Christianity" as a label for this general movement, although I recognize that there are differing streams of thinking within it. Sometimes these differing streams have competing goals and conflicting theological claims and are not nearly as unified as the general term may imply. I will discuss many of these differences in the subsequent chapters. However, one purpose of this book is to see the points of both similarity and difference while also observing the common thrust of the movement as a whole.

What do I mean by saying "gay Christianity" is the attempt to reconcile the Christian faith with homosexuality? The *Christian faith* is the body of beliefs, practices, and values—rooted in the Bible—that have defined the teaching, worship, and ministry of the Christian church throughout her existence. As briefly mentioned above, the Christian view of homosexuality has been clearly understood until recent years.

*Homosexuality* is likewise a broad term—including notions of desire, attraction, sexual behavior, relationships, identity, language, community, and culture. One aspect of the gay debate within the church is the ever-broadening definition of homosexuality within Western culture. As homosexuality is lived out by people and embraced by society, the particular meanings that may be ascribed to the concept of homosexuality change. Even the words used to describe homosexuality change over time—such as the emergence of the word *gay* as the preferred term for identifying as a homosexual.

The last element of this definition of "gay Christianity" is the word *reconcile*. *Reconcile* means to bring into harmony, to

3

settle a conflict, or to make two things consistent that were at one time inconsistent. If the Christian faith and homosexuality are seen as being at odds, then "gay Christianity" is the attempt to find some level of compatibility between them. It assumes that these two ideas are not fundamentally opposed but have points of common agreement.

This book is intended to serve as an introduction, rebuttal, and warning. It was written to help the average person in the pew to understand what is being argued by major "gay Christian" thinkers and to respond to it biblically. Although the Bible is our primary focus, we will not shy away from discussing controversial topics like homophobia, LGBT suicide rates, conversion therapy laws, and the rise of "gay celibate Christianity." Truth demands proper application to every aspect of our life and society.

There are five central ways in which "gay Christianity" is impacting the Christian church: the rethinking of theology (chapter 1), the rethinking of the Bible (chapter 2), the rethinking of the church (chapter 3), the rethinking of identity (chapter 4), and the rise of LGBT activists within the church (chapter 5). Each chapter includes a careful explanation of some facet of that problem, illustrations of how these things have been seen, and guidance for understanding these issues in light of scripture. A list of recommended resources that may help further inquiry is included at the end.

As we navigate these treacherous waters, we must be careful and discerning. Like other forms of LGBT activism, "gay Christianity" is a complex and constantly shifting concern. It is restless and relentless. Terms change, emphases shift, and subtle challenges are brought in. It can, at times, sound quite agreeable—as if the only ones truly concerned about Christian love and church unity are those who support "gay Christianity." But we must look deeper than the surface claims of inclusion and justice to understand whether these statements are truly biblical.

Whether you realize it or not, these topics are shaping pastors, church leaders, seminary professors, and ministry heads. Through social media, many ideas from "gay Christianity" are finding their way into the mainstream. They are being used to challenge common people in conservative churches, to chastise them for their traditional values, and to force them either to rethink their beliefs or to remain silent. You may find that some of these ideas have slipped unnoticed into your church or denomination. You may also find unexpected ways that your own thinking has been subtly influenced by arguments from "gay Christian" activists.

For those concerned about honoring God with your lives, I hope and pray that this book stirs you to think about the threat "gay Christianity" poses to the church and the world. I hope it renews your thinking because it presents the Word of God clearly and applies the truth accurately. That is my goal.

## A Caution before Reading

*But he [Jesus] answered, "It is written, 'Man shall not live by bread alone, but by every word that comes from the mouth of God.'"* — Matthew 4:4

If you find yourself dismissive of the scriptural claims put forward in this book, I ask you to honestly consider why. Have you embraced worldly thinking that keeps you from taking God at His word? Do you have unconfessed sexual sin that makes you feel like a hypocrite for speaking against homosexuality? Are you embarrassed by the claims of the Bible because of how it makes you look to nonbelievers? Do you crave the praise of worldly friends? Are you trying to find a way to make homosexuality acceptable because of someone you care about?

"Gay Christianity" puts forth many arguments, but the main reason people capitulate, compromise, rethink, and turn away from biblical teaching on these issues is that the cost of following Christ is simply too high. They think there must be an easier way, a more loving way, a more just way. "Gay Christianity" claims to offer a way to do all of that without jettisoning Jesus at all. They forget that the same Jesus who said we should love our neighbor (Mark 12:28–30) also said that the gate that leads to life is narrow and few are those who find it (Matthew 7:13–14). They forget that Jesus defined love toward Him this way: "Whoever has my commandments and keeps them, he it is who loves me. And he who loves me will be loved by my Father, and I will love him and manifest myself to him" (John 14:21).

Christian: Let's renew our confidence in God. His Word is true. We have no reason to doubt it or adjust it. As we look into these controversial topics and the ways they have infiltrated or impacted Christian thinking, we need not cower in fear. No one feels sufficient for the task of bearing witness and speaking boldly—but God has promised to give us what we need if we will walk forward in faith. As you read, I hope you will have the boldness to stand firm upon God's Word while confidently representing Christ to a lost and dying world. For He is the only hope for any of us.

*But thanks be to God, who in Christ always leads us in triumphal procession, and through us spreads the fragrance of the knowledge of him everywhere. For we are the aroma of Christ to God among those who are being saved and among those who are perishing, to one a fragrance from death to death, to the other a fragrance from life to life. Who is sufficient for these things? For we are not, like so many, peddlers of God's word, but as men of sincerity, as commissioned by God, in the sight of God we speak in Christ.*
— 2 Corinthians 2:14–17

# CHAPTER 1

# RETHINKING THEOLOGY

A major goal of "gay Christianity" is to make homosexuality acceptable within the Christian church. But how this goal is pursued—and what in particular is being argued at different points—varies. "Gay Christianity" is not a monolithic, unified whole. There are many streams of differing beliefs and emphases throughout it and within it. There are ongoing debates among "gay Christians" over how to interpret certain passages of scripture, how much to heed traditional church teaching, what an inclusive church should look like, how to understand homosexual identity, and how LGBT solidarity should function in society. Though most "gay Christianity" sits within the larger paradigm of *progressive Christianity*, there are some "gay Christians" who consider themselves theological conservatives. Even within each of these general streams of thought, there are internal variances and nuances.

Nevertheless, there are common themes that unify these differing streams of thought. "Gay Christian" theology can be broadly summarized into these three categories: affirming theology, queer theology, and gay celibate theology. These categories will help us to understand the types of debates happening in different churches and to identify where ideas may be coming from. It may also help us to see where things are headed.

## What Is Affirming Theology?

*Christians who affirm the full authority of Scripture can also affirm committed, monogamous same-sex relationships.*
— Matthew Vines, gay author and speaker[1]

**Affirming theology** (or **revisionist theology**, as some critics call it) holds that homosexual behavior is normal and acceptable, even for Christians. This means that homosexual behavior is not viewed as a sin and homosexual orientation is not seen as the result of Adam and Eve's sin in Genesis 3. Rather, homosexuality is seen as a gift from God—a reflection of God's design and an expression of His diverse creation. In this way, gay marriage is celebrated, "coming out" is encouraged, gay clergy are ordained, and LGBT activism is promoted.

When most people think about "gay Christianity," they likely have some notion of affirming theology in their minds. Perhaps they recall debates in mainline denominations like the Episcopal Church or the United Methodist Church, or perhaps they think of rainbow-colored "welcoming and affirming" signs in the front of church buildings. These are expressions of the growing influence of affirming theology.

Although it may sound ironic to conservatives, affirming

---

1. Matthew Vines, *God and the Gay Christian: The Biblical Case for Same-Sex Relationships* (New York: Convergent Books, 2014), 3.

## Current Proponents of Affirming Theology

**Matthew Vines** – founder of The Reformation Project and author of *God and the Gay Christian* (2014)

**Justin Lee** – founder of Gay Christian Network (now known as Q Christian Fellowship)

**Adam Hamilton** – ordained Methodist pastor (UMC) and author of *Making Sense of the Bible* (2014)

**Kathy Baldock** – speaker and author of *Walking the Bridge-less Canyon* (2014)

**Colby Martin** – author of *UnClobber: Rethinking Our Misuse of the Bible on Homosexuality* (2016)

**David Gushee** – ethicist at Mercer University and author of *Changing Our Minds* (2014)

theologians frequently say that the Bible is important for Christians and that it should guide their thinking in some way. Matthew Vines uses the language of scriptural authority to promote gay marriage, as in the above quotation from *God and the Gay Christian*. Likewise, Troy Perry, founder of the gay-affirming denomination Metropolitan Community Church, says that the Bible is "inspired by God" and that it "provides a key source of authority for the Christian faith"

11

while also saying that "gay men and lesbians should be accepted just as they are in Christian churches, and homosexual relationships should be celebrated and affirmed."[2] These kinds of statements obviously require a rethinking of key biblical texts that have been understood as condemnations of homosexual behavior for centuries. This rethinking is one of the major projects of affirming theology.

Therefore, affirming theologians say that the Bible truly condemns only homosexual activity that is nonconsensual (rape), exploitative (pederasty/pedophilia), or idolatrous (temple prostitution). They also say that the love ethic of the Bible overrides any potentially condemning references to homosexual behavior as long as the love between the couple is genuinely felt. Furthermore, they say that science proves that homosexual orientation is natural and that people should not feel shame for their sexual feelings. They argue that because homosexual orientation was not defined and understood until the nineteenth century, the Bible is unable to address that concern without the aid of contemporary science and the personal experiences of LGBT people within the church.

*Revisionist theology* is not a term that gay-affirming theologians give to their own work but one applied to them by conservative critics. The reason for the label is that it describes the way affirming theology approaches scriptural interpretation. Rather than taking the words of the Bible as having a particular meaning intended by the author,

---

2. Troy D. Perry and Thomas L.P. Swicegood, *Don't Be Afraid Anymore: The Story of Reverend Troy Perry and Metropolitan Community Churches* (New York, NY: St. Martin's Press, 1990), 339–340.

affirming theologians believe that newly discovered information unveils new implications in the text that have been hidden from the church for centuries. This was a frequent appeal during the gay marriage debates of the 2000s, for instance, when affirming theologians argued that Paul spoke against homosexuality because he only knew about exploitative or violent forms of homosexual behavior—he didn't know about committed, monogamous, same-sex relationships. The implication was that we know more about these things than the Apostle Paul and therefore we can better understand what he wrote than previous generations of Christians did.

It is worth noting that in the grand scheme of church history, affirming theology is a very recent phenomenon. Nevertheless, it is the oldest stream of "gay Christian" thinking, and many of the original arguments it posed are still with us today. The first affirming argument to hit the scene was in the 1955 book *Homosexuality and the Western Christian Tradition* by Church of England ethicist Derrick Sherwin Bailey, who argued that God's destruction of Sodom and Gomorrah had nothing to do with homosexuality. Instead, Bailey argued that the destruction of the ancient cities was due to their inhospitality toward strangers. This view became one of the standard revisions offered by affirming theology.

Some of the early affirming theologians took a more philosophical approach to revisionism. For example, in *Time for Consent: A Christian's Approach to Homosexuality* (1970), Anglican theologian Norman Pittenger redefined humanity, sin, and God's law away from historic Christian definitions.

For Pittenger, the central truth about man is that "he is *created to be* and *is a lover*."[3] With this new definition of humanity in place, he argued that homosexual sex acts are not inherently wicked because they are merely expressions of love. If human beings were created to give and receive love, then the church should allow homosexuals to express their love in the way that feels most natural to them.

As gay activism became more pronounced, the 1970s saw a number of American books that sought to reconcile homosexuality with the Christian faith. Here is a sampling:

- Troy Perry's *The Lord Is My Shepherd and He Knows I'm Gay* (1972) and Malcolm Boyd's *Take Off the Masks* (1978) are memoirs from Christian ministers who saw their homosexuality as blessed by God.

- John J. McNeill's *The Church and the Homosexual* (1976) and Letha Scanzoni and Virginia Ramey Mollenkott's *Is the Homosexual My Neighbor?* (1978) challenged the Christian church to rethink its doctrine in order to be more accepting of homosexuals.

- Tom Horner's *Jonathan Loved David: Homosexuality in Biblical Times* (1976) created a direct challenge to the biblical passages concerning homosexuality while also offering a new interpretation of Jonathan and David's relationship.

---

3. Norman Pittenger, *Time for Consent: A Christian's Approach to Homosexuality* (London: SCM Press, 1970), 43.

- James B. Nelson's *Embodiment: An Approach to Sexuality and Christian Theology* (1978), building extensively upon Norman Pittenger's work, sought a comprehensive rethinking of Christian sexual ethics. Nelson's writing proved particularly influential in the already shifting stance of the United Church of Christ toward affirming homosexuality.

Many of these writings laid the basic framework of affirming arguments going forward. They would be frequently cited in denominational study committee reports and other religious presentations that questioned the church's response to homosexuality, same-sex marriage, and gay ordination. Yet the most widely influential book was yet to come.

Yale Historian John Boswell's *Christianity, Social Tolerance, and Homosexuality: Gay People in Western Europe from the Beginning of the Christian Era to the Fourteenth Century* (1980) represented a major rethinking of theology, church history, and Christian values. Boswell's thesis was that Christianity was not fundamentally intolerant of homosexuality. Rather, he claimed, prior to the twelfth century AD, Christianity had tolerated and sometimes celebrated it. He argued that anti-gay bias crept in during the Middle Ages due to Thomas Aquinas and a few others who steered the church away from its original, more tolerant course. Boswell stated that the purpose of his book was to rebut the idea that Christian belief was "the cause of intolerance in regards to gay people."[4]

---

4. John Boswell, *Christianity, Social Tolerance, and Homosexuality: Gay People in Western Europe from the Beginning of the Christian Era to the Fourteenth Century* (Chicago, IL: The University of Chicago Press, 1980), 6.

It was an intriguing counterargument to the conservative position. Boswell's book was cleverly designed to cast doubt on the assumption that the church had been historically unified in its teaching on homosexual behavior. While his main appeal was to various historic sources, Boswell also offered a detailed reinterpretation of the relevant biblical passages on homosexuality—whittling them down to irrelevancies by disconnecting them from the larger ethical framework of scripture.

For instance, Boswell accepted Derrick Sherwin Bailey's 1955 interpretation of Sodom's destruction, dismissed Leviticus as completely irrelevant to the discussion, cast doubt on the exact meaning of Paul's language in the New Testament, and said, "Sexuality appears to have been largely a matter of indifference to Jesus."[5] He concluded his overview of scriptural teaching by saying, "The New Testament takes no demonstrable position on homosexuality."[6]

The *New York Times* and *Newsweek* heralded the book as a breakthrough, and *Christianity, Social Tolerance, and Homosexuality* won the National Book Award for History in 1981. It gained a wide readership and became required reading in many college courses and seminary classes—becoming the go-to text for the next generation of affirming theologians. Plenty of other affirming works have been written since Boswell, but none have been able to match the influence his book had on the debate both inside and outside the church.

---

5. Ibid., 114.
6. Ibid., 117.

## What Is Queer Theology?

*The God of my queer faith is a wildly inclusive Spirit who creates ever-expanding diversity and loves everyone, regardless of sexual orientation or gender identity. I see God disrupting all attempts to be defined or confined—how queer!* — Kittredge Cherry, lesbian minister and writer[7]

**Queer theology** holds that *queerness* should be celebrated by liberating it from the confines of traditional thinking. *Queer* used to be considered a pejorative term, but many members of the LGBT community now happily use it as a personal or group label. As a personal label, someone may identify as *queer* if they think that the terms *gay* or *lesbian* are too limiting (hence the inclusion of Q in the fuller LGBTQ+ acronym). As an idea, *queerness* is an umbrella term for anything falling outside of heterosexual or stereotypical gender norms. *Queer* also takes on a more combative and transgressive tone when used in academic studies—such as queer theory and queer theology. *Transgression* is an important theme in queer theory, as it is the expression of crossing set boundaries and pushing against social norms.

With this in mind, *queer theology* is a radical push against boundaries and expectations. While *affirming theology* is essentially an attempt to reconcile Christianity with homosexual practice, *queer theology* has no such reconciliation in

---

7. Kittredge Cherry, "My Queer Faith Calls Me to Be a Virtual Voice in the Wilderness," *Q Spirit*, February 7, 2018, http://qspirit.net/queer-theology-faith-virtual-voice/.

## Current Proponents of Queer Theology

**Patrick S. Cheng** – ordained Episcopal priest and author of *Radical Love: An Introduction of Queer Theology* (2011)

**Shannon T.L. Kearns** – ordained Old Catholic priest and cofounder of QueerTheology.com

**Kittredge Cherry** – author of *Jesus in Love: A Novel* (2006) and founder of QSpirit.net

**Robert E. Shore-Goss** – author of *Jesus Acted Up* (1993) and *Queering Christ* (2002)

**Dianna E. Anderson** – author of *Damaged Goods: New Perspectives on Christian Purity* (2015)

view. It sees its purpose as one of disruption, defiance, resistance, and liberation from what is called *heteronormativity* (the worldview that heterosexuality is normal and good). As queer theologian Robert Shore-Goss says, queer theology arises from "a practice of resistance, conflict, and struggle for liberation" in an attempt to "free biblical discourse from the distortions of heterosexist/homophobic power."[8] In that way it has deep connections with both *liberation theology* and *feminist theology*, not to mention *queer theory*. Because of the

---

8. Robert Goss, *Jesus Acted Up: A Gay and Lesbian Manifesto* (New York, NY: HarperCollins Publishers, 1993), 88.

complicated academic streams that feed into queer theology, a few definitions are necessary.

*Liberation theology,* a movement that began in Latin America, has had a profound effect on Christian thinking in the twentieth and twenty-first centuries all over the world. As theological historian Alistair McGrath explains, "Liberation theology is oriented toward the poor and oppressed. It involves critical reflection on practice, and should not be detached from social involvement or political action."[9] This emphasis on "the oppressed" as a unique class of people is a crucial idea in liberation theology. By reading the biblical text through the lens of the oppressed, theologians use their theology as a means of social action—working to liberate the oppressed from their "oppressors." As academics have used liberation theology to redefine the Christian faith, adherents to orthodox teaching have increasingly been represented as the oppressors—dismissed as those upholding systems of power, oppression, exploitation, and abuse.

*Feminist theology* helped further apply the oppressor/oppressed framework of liberation theology to other social groups—particularly women. Elisabeth Schüssler Fiorenza, a feminist theologian, describes this subjective interpretive principle this way: "To truly understand the Bible is to read it through the eyes of the oppressed since the God who speaks in the Bible is the God of the oppressed."[10] Of course, the oppressed in the liberationist sense are not widows and orphans (James 1:27) or even the poor per se, but anyone

---

9. Alistair McGrath, *The Christian Theology Reader: 25th Anniversary Fifth Edition* (Hoboken, NJ: Wiley Blackwell, 2016), 54.

10. Elisabeth Schüssler Fiorenza, *Bread Not Stone: The Challenge of Feminist Biblical Interpretation* (Boston, MA: Beacon Press, 1984), 50.

who lacks political and social power—particularly women, ethnic minorities, and LGBT people. Queer theology took these ideas and ran with them.

Assimilation into a religious system that prioritizes and prizes the natural family, for instance, is not the goal of queer theology. Rather, the goal is tearing down all the theology and social expectations that undergird the priority of the natural family in Christian teaching in order to rebuild a system that celebrates the "open frontier" that the word *queer* implies.[11] This, queer theologians claim, is the kind of liberation the church should be striving for.

Through its connection with *queer theory*, queer theology frequently becomes a project of postmodern *literary deconstruction* (the idea that all texts have inherent contradictions and that meaning is found in these contradictions). One way this deconstruction is expressed is through a process known as *queering* (or *queer reading*), where "queer experience" is playfully read into a text or theological idea in order to present new subversive possibilities and to frustrate traditional readings.

More will be said about this practice in chapter 3, but a very basic example of queering would be to take the theological formulation of "one God in three persons" we know as the Trinity and to call it a "divine orgy," as queer theologian Marcella Althaus-Reid does.[12] This is not a statement of belief so much as it is a poetic statement intended to shock

---

11. Mark Larrimore, introduction to *Queer Christianities: Lived Religion in Transgressive Forms*, eds. Kathleen T. Talvacchia, Michael F. Pettinger, and Mark Larrimore (New York and London: New York University Press, 2015), 6.

12. Marcella Althaus-Reid, *The Queer God* (New York and London: Routledge, 2003), 33.

orthodox Christians and present a new possibility in the reader's imagination. A new possibility born in a reader's imagination might be how Brian G. Murphy takes this "trinity as orgy" idea when he blasphemously says, "But if the trinity is an orgy, maybe we don't have to feel bad about our sexual desires. . . . [We can] go proudly to that sex party, because God is an orgy."[13]

Obviously, queer theology's commitment to disruption and noncategorization makes it difficult to clearly define— which also makes it incoherent as a distinct systematic theology. But it does make it effective as a force of disruption. As Robert Shore-Goss triumphantly declares:

*Fundamentalist and literalist Christians traffic in the production and commerce of certain truths, but doubts, ambiguities, pluralities, and complexities will bring their fragile discursive edifice of fundamentalist truth to an end in the area of public discourse and curtail its harmful effect to those who are sexually different.*[14]

This is the goal of queer theology: total destruction of orthodoxy. While we might traditionally think of theology as an attempt to articulate and categorize objective spiritual truths, in queer theology, truth is basically irrelevant. The purpose is not clarity but "doubts, ambiguities, pluralities,

---

13. Brian G. Murphy, "What Promiscuity Taught Me about God's Love." Queer Theology, https://www.queertheology.com/what-promiscuity-taught-me-about-gods-love/.

14. Robert Goss, *Jesus Acted Up: A Gay and Lesbian Manifesto* (New York, NY: HarperCollins Publishers, 1993), 101.

and complexities" that operate as their own weapons against God's truth.

Because of this, the lines between affirming theology and queer theology are not always obvious. A previous generation's affirming theology may become the next generation's queer theology if the tasks of subversion and liberation are taken up. In this way, queer theology becomes more than a theoretical academic exercise; it is a way of practically transgressing the boundaries of orthodoxy and good taste.

## What Is Gay Celibate Theology?

*The experience of same-sex desire may be the divinely appointed way in which celibate gay Christians discover the power of Christ made perfect in their lives.* — Wesley Hill, gay celibate author[15]

**Gay celibate theology** (or **Side B theology**, as it is sometimes called) is the more conservative stream of "gay Christian" thinking which holds to the traditional teaching that the Bible forbids *homosexual behavior* but also believes that the Bible is silent concerning *homosexual orientation*, or what is sometimes called *same-sex attraction*. In this view, same-sex attraction is not seen as sinful and therefore not something a Christian must repent of or feel any shame about. Rather, same-sex attraction becomes a unique burden that a "gay Christian" must personally steward with the

---

15. Wesley Hill, *Washed and Waiting: Reflections on Christian Faithfulness and Homosexuality* (Grand Rapids, MI: Zondervan, 2010), 201.

## Proponents of Gay Celibate Theology

**Wesley Hill** – author of *Washed and Waiting* (2010) and *Spiritual Friendship* (2015)

**Nate Collins** – founder of Revoice and author of *All But Invisible* (2017)

**Ed Shaw** – cofounder of Living Out and author of *Same-Sex Attraction and the Church* (2015)

**Greg Johnson** – ordained pastor in the Presbyterian Church in America (PCA)

**Bridget Eileen Rivera** – blogger and author of *Heavy Burdens* (2021)

**Preston Sprinkle** – president of The Center for Faith, Sexuality & Gender and author of *People to Be Loved* (2015)

encouragement of the church. It is called *gay celibate theology* because of its emphasis on celibacy as opposed to homosexual relationships. The label can be a bit of misnomer, however, because there are some who hold to Side B thinking who have married an opposite-sex spouse in what is called *mixed-orientation marriage.*

Side B theology is built upon the twin pillars of secular psychology and identity theory. This is why it emphasizes the immutability of sexual orientation (in other words, a gay person will not be able to become straight) and the importance of gay Christians cultivating their sexual identity along with their personal faith (even though, ironically, their sexual identity will not be expressed sexually).

According to psychologist and Side B proponent Mark Yarhouse:

> *From a Christian perspective, if God's revealed will is that full genital sexual contact should occur only in the context of a life-long heterosexual union, then same-sex behavior is the primary concern rather than same-sex attraction or orientation. If neither attractions nor orientation change, the sexual ethic remains, so believers must take responsibility for whether and how they express their impulses in their behavior.*[16]

In his view, what is needed is for Christians to develop a more nuanced understanding of *sexual identity* because "the church has not offered a particularly compelling vision for identity in light of the experiences of sexual minorities.[17]

In its more theoretical configuration, gay celibate theology has attempted to define *sexual orientation* as a *disability* rather than a temptation, sin pattern, or sinful condition. Nate Collins makes this point plain in his book *All But Invisible* (2017):

---

16. Mark A. Yarhouse, "A Christian Perspective on Sexual Identity," Carl F.H. Henry Center for Theological Understanding | TEDS, January 1, 2010, 10, https://henrycenter.tiu.edu/resource/a-christian-perspective-on-sexual-identity/.

17. Ibid., 18.

*As I've contemplated my own experience as a gay man and talked with hundreds of other gay men and women over the years, I've decided that the term disability is the most helpful theological category to understand how gay people experience the effects of both the fall and redemption on their orientations.*[18]

The newly emerging field of disability theology has become a major jumping-off point for some Side B writers. *Disability theology* is a stream of theological inquiry that focuses on the experiences of the impaired or disabled. Because of its roots in liberation theology, disability theology sees disabled people as an oppressed people group who have been harmed more by society than by their personal impairment.[19] Traditional theological concepts such as healing, wholeness, original sin, and human flourishing are reassessed in light of disabled experience. Gay celibate theologians have compared themselves to people born with disabilities—offering a similar emphasis on social acceptance and accessibility.

Despite some of its headier academic influences, gay celibate theology works primarily as a practical theology of how conservative "gay Christians" should live and how the conservative church should make space for them without trying to "fix" or "cure" them. By emphasizing the negative impact of conservative teaching on LGBT people, it assumes that conservatives have gotten a lot of things wrong about

18. Nate Collins, *All But Invisible: Exploring Identity Questions at the Intersection of Faith, Gender, and Sexuality* (Grand Rapids, MI: Zondervan, 2017), 190–191.

19. Rebecca S. Chopp, foreword to *The Disabled God: Toward a Liberation Theology of Disability* by Nancy L. Eiesland (Nashville, TN: Abingdon Press, 1994), 9.

homosexuality that need to be corrected. Side B proponent Preston Sprinkle states as much in the preface to *People to Be Loved*:

> *We're going to hold our views with a humble heart and an open hand—inviting God to correct us where we have been wrong. We are going to do our best to lay aside our assumptions and genuinely seek to know what the Bible, not our tradition, says about homosexuality.*[20]

As many Side B proponents admit, they do not see the Christian's task as providing biblical answers to these questions; rather, the Christian's job is to listen to LGBT experience so as to better facilitate a conversation. For example, Preston Sprinkle continues his preface by saying:

> *This book reflects an ongoing conversation with many people about the Bible, the church, and homosexuality. The word* ongoing *is important. This book is not my last word on homosexuality, but my first word (in print, at least). It doesn't represent my codified, unchangeable, etched-in-stone declaration of what I have and always will believe about homosexuality. This book is a contribution to a complex conversation about a difficult topic. I would be in sin if I had the audacity to declare that I have it all figured out.*[21]

Mark Yarhouse laid much of the groundwork for gay celibate theology with his psychological writing dating back

---

20. Preston Sprinkle, *People to Be Loved* (Grand Rapids, MI: Zondervan, 2015), 10.
21. Ibid., 11.

to the early 2000s. The distinction between Side A (affirming) and Side B (celibate or nonaffirming) initially came out of internet dialogue on the Gay Christian Network between these "two types of gay Christians" throughout the decade.[22]

In 2010, Wesley Hill, a graduate of Wheaton College, emerged as the most important trailblazer in gay celibate thinking with the book *Washed and Waiting: Reflections on Christian Faithfulness and Homosexuality* (2010). Hill's memoir described his own inner conflict regarding his homosexuality and his celibacy. "This book is about . . . how, practically, a nonpracticing but still-desiring homosexual Christian can 'prove, live out, and celebrate' the grace of Christ and the power of the Holy Spirit *in homosexual terms*."[23] Hill's book added a new wrinkle to evangelical writing on the subject: Christians should stop expecting gay people to change and instead offer their empathy and support. In this paradigm, *gay* and *Christian* were no longer competing identity labels but coexisting experiences.

Many evangelicals were attracted to Hill's emphasis on personal devotion rather than overcoming homosexual temptation, his willingness to dialogue with affirming authors like Justin Lee rather than debate them, his soft tone toward LGBT people rather than the aggressive sociopolitical tone of the culture wars, and the charitable middle road he offered between affirming theology and strident fundamentalism. Despite objections to Hill's use of terms

---

22. Gay Christian Network, web archive snapshot, June 13, 2008, https://web.archive.org/web/20080613054152/http://www.gaychristiannetwork.com/.

23. Wesley Hill, *Washed and Waiting: Reflections on Christian Faithfulness and Homosexuality* (Grand Rapids, MI: Zondervan, 2010), 16. (Emphasis belongs to original author.)

like *homosexual Christian*, mainstream evangelicals such as Tim Keller, The Gospel Coalition, *Christianity Today*, *SBC Voices*, and many evangelical blogs favorably reviewed *Washed and Waiting*, and Hill became a frequent guest speaker at Christian college campuses.

In 2012, Wesley Hill and fellow gay celibate theologian Ron Belgau founded *SpiritualFriendship.org*, a blog for Side B writers who were frustrated with "the prevailing narratives about homosexuality from those who embrace this traditionally Christian sexual ethic: an excessive focus on political issues, and the ubiquity of reparative therapy in one form or another."[24] The blog became a minicompendium of the theology, philosophy, preoccupations, frustrations, observations, and personal stories of gay celibate Christians. Hill would go on to write *Spiritual Friendship: Finding Love in the Church as a Celibate Gay Christian* (2015), a book that encouraged committed celibate partnerships as a Side B alternative to gay marriage.

Across the 2010s, other books that shaped Side B theology included Jenell Williams Paris's *The End of Sexual Identity* (2011), Preston Sprinkle's *People to Be Loved* (2015), Andrew Marin's *Us Versus Us: The Untold Story of Religion and the LGBT Community* (2016), Gregory Coles's *Single Gay Christian* (2017), Nate Collins's *All But Invisible* (2017), and Mark Yarhouse and Olya Zaporozhets's *Costly Obedience: What We Can Learn from the Celibate Gay Christian Community* (2019).

24. "About," Spiritual Friendship, web archive snapshot, October 22, 2012. https://web.archive.org/web/20121022012404/http://spiritualfriendship.org/about/.

But it was the 2018 promotion of the Side B-focused Revoice Conference in St. Louis that brought the questions of gay celibate theology to the forefront in many churches. Hosted in a Presbyterian Church in America (PCA) church and founded by graduates of Southern Baptist Theological Seminary (Nate Collins) and Covenant Theological Seminary (Stephen Moss), the conference was billed under the mission of "supporting, encouraging, and empowering" LGBT Christians who were committed to orthodox teaching.[25] The controversy over Revoice highlighted that gay celibate theology, unbeknownst to many, had found a significant hearing in conservative churches, especially among the younger generation of pastors, campus ministers, and church planters.

## Legitimate Biblical Interpretation

*Do your best to present yourself to God as one approved, a worker who has no need to be ashamed, rightly handling the word of truth.* — 2 Timothy 2:15

If there is one thing that will guide this discussion more than anything else, it is the way a person approaches the scriptures. We recognize intuitively that different approaches will lead to different outcomes. If one person reads a statement as being *literally true* while another person reads a statement as being *figuratively true*, for instance, we would expect them

---

25. Revoice 2018, web archive snapshot, June 15, 2018, https://web.archive.org/web/20180615231009/https://revoice.us/.

to apply that statement in different ways because they understand the statement in different ways. But the issue that plagues our society is the assumption that all interpretations are equally valid. This is simply not true. Christians must be clear about the right and proper way to interpret the Bible, or we will be led into all kinds of doctrinal error and harmful life applications.

It may seem like common sense to many Bible-believing Christians, but as apologist Richard Howe explains, we should use a method of interpretation "that uses the normal grammar of the writing and the historical context of the author and audience to discover the meaning of the text."[26] This is called the *grammatical/historical method*. Using this method helps ensure that we are remaining faithful to what the biblical author intended to communicate and not reading into the text what we would like the author to have communicated. Whether or not we are fluent in the original languages of ancient Hebrew or Greek, the grammatical/historical method can help us stay true to the author's intention in writing.

One of the sad by-products of the rise of postmodernism is not just the general relativizing of truth but the undermining of authorial intent in particular. Literary theorists have shaken our confidence that anyone can truly decipher the intent of an author at all. Even worse, they have minimized the importance of an author's intention in our understanding of a text. In its place, theorists have put forward the notion that *reader-response criticism* (which prioritizes the reactions

---

26. Richard G. Howe, *Intro to God's Revelation: 6 Week Curriculum Workbook* (Tupelo, MS: American Family Association, 2018), 61.

of readers) is essential to our interpretation of a text.

As one postmodern Bible scholar explains it:

> *The postmodern perspective which allows readers to use the Bible today is that of a radical reader-oriented literary criticism, a criticism which views literature in terms of readers and their values, attitudes, and responses. This supplements and relativizes views of literature in terms of the universe imitated in the work, the author, the audience, and the work itself.*[27]

In other words, in postmodernism, the written text is not tied to the author's intentions but is subject to the values and perspectives a reader brings to it. Even for the Bible.

We sometimes forget that the fundamental reason a person speaks or writes is to communicate something that will be understood. That basic principle is behind God—the ultimate Author—giving us His Word. It is also true for each individual author whom God chose to write the books of the Old and New Testaments. They are part of a text intended to communicate a consistent and understandable message with a notable spiritual outcome on the Christian reader or hearer: "All Scripture is breathed out by God and profitable for teaching, for reproof, for correction, and for training in righteousness, that the man of God may be complete, equipped for every good work" (2 Timothy 3:16–17). The fact that the text was written in a different language, time period, and culture than our own only adds some potential

---

27. Edgar V. McKnight, *Postmodern Use of the Bible: The Emergence of Reader-Oriented Criticism* (Nashville, TN: Abingdon Press, 1988), 14–15.

hurdles to our immediate understanding; it does not make the task of understanding utterly impossible.

Christians should be wary of the objection often given by skeptics and progressives that there is no such thing as an authoritative interpretation of biblical passages—especially in the debate over homosexuality. As we shall see in the next chapter, scripture really is clear on these issues. As much as some people may want to raise an objection or think that the very existence of an alternate, progressive viewpoint means the passages are unclear, if they treat the scriptural text fairly and assume God is consistent and intentional in what He says, they will find the answer—even if they don't like it. Having read dozens of arguments that treat the Bible skeptically, I can say that one axiom holds true: if you want the Bible to be unclear on a subject, you can always find a way to make it unclear.

One other aspect of legitimate biblical interpretation is to remember that the Bible is sufficient to teach us who God is and how we should live before Him (Psalm 19:7). We need no other source, and every other source that might tell us anything true must be in alignment with scripture. This is also taught in 2 Timothy 3. Part of the completion and equipping promised to the man of God assumes that the scriptures are what is being used to teach, reproof, correct, and train in righteousness.

The sources to which "gay Christians" constantly appeal—secular psychology, sociological data, identity theory, and the personal experiences of people who identify as sexual minorities—are not sufficient to guide us into all truth. They are where the world looks for answers because the world is blind. "The natural person does not accept the things of the Spirit of God, for they are folly to him, and he is not able to understand them because they are spiritually discerned" (1 Corinthians 2:14).

One LGBT affirming pastor—after spending 28 pages and over 14,000 words arguing against the traditional interpretation of scripture—summarized his approach to the Bible quite succinctly: "When in doubt, err on the side of human experience."[28]

This book is *not* about erring on the side of human experience. What makes human experience a sure guide to truth anyway? How many times might we reinterpret our own experiences over the course of our lives? How well do we truly know ourselves? As that quote illustrates, our worldview is deeply shaped by our view of authority. If the Bible is God's holy, inerrant, and clear revelation, then it is the foundation of all that we should believe and do—regardless of anyone's contrary personal experience. The response at that point is either to submit ourselves to the truth or reject what it says.

---

28. D. Mark Davis, "Letters to Jerri: On the Bible and Same-Sex Marriage," Covenant Network of Presbyterians, January 19, 2016, https://covnetpres.org/wp-content/uploads/sites/71/2016/01/Letters-to-Jerri-by-D.-Mark-Davis.pdf.

## What's the Problem?

*Thus says the Lord: "Let not the wise man boast in his wisdom, let not the mighty man boast in his might, let not the rich man boast in his riches, but let him who boasts boast in this, that he understands and knows me, that I am the Lord who practices steadfast love, justice, and righteousness in the earth. For in these things I delight, declares the Lord."* — Jeremiah 9:23–24

It is important to remember that the purpose of **Christian theology** is to know God. Because the Bible is where we learn with certainty who God is and what He has done, we can further understand *Christian theology* as an explanation of what the Bible teaches. How we get to the overall teaching of the Bible is through proper interpretation—that is, interpretation that adheres to the words and statements of scripture. Any thoughts, observations, impressions, experiences, and feelings we have must be weighed and judged in light of what scripture says, not the other way around. "Gay Christianity" gets this backward.

**Affirming theology** seeks to *revise* the established teaching of the Bible by first considering what LGBT people want to hear. Though the scripture is clear on its face, affirming theologians introduce doubt and suspicion, slyly suggesting that there are layers of cultural context that have been missed for centuries. It uses the scripture to present LGBT orientations as wholesome and holy. This deception is in direct opposition to God's design for human sexuality and scripture's warnings about such people being outside the kingdom of God.

**Queer theology** wants to *deconstruct* the boundaries of orthodoxy to make theology scandalous to conservatives. It is not a serious study of scripture or of God Himself but a proclamation of defiant transgression—a project where God and His Word are simply literary symbols held up to the twisted imaginations of people who hate Him. Believing theology to be a tool of self-empowerment rather than understanding, it moves beyond affirmation to full-on scoffing. "But you must remember, beloved, the predictions of the apostles of our Lord Jesus Christ. They said to you, 'In the last time there will be scoffers, following their own ungodly passions.' It is these who cause divisions, worldly people, devoid of the Spirit" (Jude 1:17–19).

**Gay celibate theology** wants to *essentialize* homosexual temptation to the point that it is left untouched by the work of the Holy Spirit. "Gay Christian," "LGBT Christian," "same-sex attracted Christian," and "sexual minority" are considered valid and useful identity labels, and Christians who resist those labels are seen as homophobic. Though gay celibate theologians claim to hold to the historic Christian sexual ethic, they import ideas of "sexual identity" from contemporary psychology that become either variations on or subtle critiques of historic interpretation. The Bible suddenly has nothing outright to say about *homosexuality*, they argue; it now speaks only to *homosexual behavior*. Then the personal experiences of "sexual minorities" become the guide to how the church should address homosexuality as a whole—whether they profess faith or not.

It should be noted that the reason "LGBT Christianity" exists is that the psychiatric and psychological institutions have legitimized the concept of "sexual orientation"—the idea that our attractions and sexual desires are set from birth. This is a result of seeing sexual activity as a purely biological function that has no inherent meaning apart from self-expression. Our true selves, it is argued, should not be hindered in any way—certainly not in sexual fulfillment. This narrative has been enshrined in higher education and is a functional reality in our culture. People are expected to embrace their "true self" as lesbian, gay, bisexual, transgender, or queer while at the same time embracing some form of Christian religiosity.

Of course, this commitment to sexual identity can be present even if sexual expression is foregone. Consider the way gay celibate theologians speak of the particular *costliness* of celibacy for those who are same-sex attracted. As Carl Trueman observes:

*Only in a world in which selves are typically recognized or validated by their sexuality and their sexual fulfillment—in which these things define who people are at a deep level—can celibacy really be considered costly. Further, only in a world in which sexual identities—and specifically nonheterosexual sexual identities—enjoy particular cultural cachet will the celibacy of one particular group be designated as somehow especially hard or sacrificial. Traditional Christian sexual morality calls for celibacy for all who are not married and chastity for those who are. It is, strictly speaking, no more costly or sacrificial for a single person not to have sex with*

*someone than it is for a married person to be faithful or not
visit strip clubs and prostitutes.*[29]

We might think of obedience in terms of *cost* mostly if
we don't want to obey or feel a different path is deserved. But
one of the fruits of Christian maturity and genuine life by
the Holy Spirit is not merely a commitment to obey Christ
but also a joy in following Him. "For this is the love of God,
that we keep his commandments. And his commandments
are not burdensome" (1 John 5:3). This is undermined by the
focus upon and cultivation of gay sexual identity—even by
those who profess to follow the historic Christian teaching
on sexuality.

These "gay Christian" theologies may be varied, but they
are assaults on God's intention in creation and God's Word
as written. They diminish the church of Jesus Christ and
sow confusion. They attempt to elevate human reasoning
and experience above the scriptures, having them direct our
theological understanding. Love and truth are redefined.
The majesty of God is minimized, and the holiness of God
is outright blasphemed. The sin of homosexuality becomes
nuanced or is dismissed entirely. And the conviction of the
gospel is replaced with affirmation, celebration, and self-
actualization. When we are wrong in our understanding of
God, we will be led astray in many other areas.

Personal experience is not discounted entirely in
Christian theology; we need to be able to apply God's Word

---

29. Carl R. Trueman, *The Rise and Triumph of the Modern Self: Cultural Amnesia,
Expressive Individualism, and the Road to Sexual Revolution* (Wheaton, IL: Crossway,
2020), 391.

accurately. But Christians recognize that the subjectivity of experience gives us no automatic guide to truth. Everything we experience must be weighed against the scripture and understood through its teaching. And where our interpretation of experience doesn't seem to match, we must be willing to submit ourselves to the scripture rather than our own intellect. "Let God be true though every one were a liar, as it is written, 'That you may be justified in your words, and prevail when you are judged" (Romans 3:4). As Christians, our primary concern should be the character of God—and questioning the integrity of His Word is the first step toward impugning the character of God.

# CHAPTER 2

# RETHINKING THE BIBLE

What the Bible says about sex and marriage is not a mystery. But something has happened since the sexual revolution—people have suddenly found the Bible to no longer be clear on such things. Questions are raised; doubt and suspicion creep in. None of this rethinking is the result of new earth-shaking discoveries in archaeology or new biblical texts. It is the result of concerted LGBT activism that makes Christians into bigots and the plain reading of scripture into a form of hate speech. This is part of the revisionist intent of affirming theology.

The Bible refers directly to homosexuality six times. Activists have come to label these verses the "clobber passages" because, they say, the verses are used by conservatives to "clobber" the opposition and beat up on gay people. How can six measly verses really determine whether homosexuality is sinful or not? After all, shouldn't Christians be generous and loving like Jesus? Jesus didn't even say anything about homosexuality. These emotional arguments are very palatable to immature Christians. But, as we shall see, the biblical understanding of sexuality is not built from a handful of questionable passages.

The "clobber passages" are clear in their individual contexts, but in order to know what the Bible teaches about homosexuality, we must also understand the broader context of how the Bible speaks of sex in general. No command or warning is given in isolation. It all fits as part of a cohesive and clear picture of God's intention for humankind.

## The Foundation of Biblical Sexuality

*In the beginning God created the heavens and the earth.*
— Genesis 1:1

Genesis 1:1 isn't just a nice beginning to a story; it's a theological statement about the world. God made it. He designed it. He has authority over it and everything in it. Some people wonder how Christians can have such specific and limited views of sex, marriage, and family. The easy answer is "the Bible says so." But *how* the Bible says so is not as easy as opening the Bible to the book of Marriage and Family and following its guidelines. We have to look at the Bible's worldview—the framework of thinking and intention that undergirds how things are written and how they are intended to be understood.

The book of Genesis is crucial because it establishes God's pattern and plan. It describes the way God designed the world to function before sin marred everything. The order and method (and even how God *didn't* do things) all speak to God's intention. For example, because God rests on the seventh day, we have a day set apart for rest and worship.

Though God will affirm this later in the Ten Commandments, He establishes the Sabbath pattern in creation itself. This is often how God works in scripture. The way in which things happen is meaningful.

In His ordering of creation, God made human beings last. Why? Because human beings are the pinnacle of God's creation—the only ones that have been privileged with bearing God's image. This speaks to the worth of human life. This is why we should value human life above animal and plant life. It doesn't mean that other types of life-forms are meaningless or should be disregarded; it's a matter of priority and emphasis. This also means there is a moral dimension to humanity that isn't there with other life-forms.

God made man and placed him in the garden. But it is God who looked at the man and decided that despite everything around him being good, there was something that was not good—man alone. "Then the Lord God said, 'It is not good that the man should be alone; I will make him a helper fit for him'" (Genesis 2:18).

This certainly speaks to the relational nature of humanity and our need for friendship. But more directly, it establishes the institution of marriage because God's response to this situation is to create one who is like the man but different. Instead of creating the woman in the same way He made the man (from the dust), God creates her from the man's side. Then the scripture gives us this explanation: "Therefore a man shall leave his father and his mother and hold fast to his wife, and they shall become one flesh" (Genesis 2:24).

Sexual consummation in natural marriage is the reunion of these two separate yet complementary beings. It is an act of bonding and physical intimacy. Genesis 2:24 emphasizes the oneness of this union when it says, "Therefore a man shall leave his father and his mother and hold fast to his wife, and they shall become one flesh." It is also biologically designed by God to be an essential step toward fulfilling the mandate to "be fruitful and multiply" (Genesis 1:22). This unity of spirit and bodies is reflected at the end of Genesis 2: "And the man and his wife were both naked and were not ashamed" (Genesis 2:25).

In the New Testament, when Paul teaches on the roles of husbands and wives, he refers back to Genesis 2 in emphasizing what God intended marriage to signify. "'Therefore a man shall leave his father and mother and hold fast to his wife, and the two shall become one flesh.'This mystery is profound, and I am saying that it refers to Christ and the church"(Ephesians 5:31–32). For Paul, the pattern of creation has theological importance because the union of husband and wife is illustrative of Christ's union with his people. Theologian Wayne Grudem says that Adam and Eve "were *created* to represent that relationship, and that is what Paul says *all marriages* are supposed to do."[1]

Likewise, we see that Jesus' sexual ethics come out of the same Genesis passage when He says in Matthew 19:4, "Have you not read that he who created them from the beginning made them male and female?" He grounds natural marriage in God's will—noting that there is a providential purpose in being male and female. Notice too that their sexuality is defined by their biology, not by their desires. Our biological

---

1. Wayne Grudem, *Christian Ethics: An Introduction to Biblical Moral Reasoning* (Wheaton, IL: Crossway, 2018), 705.

sex not only determines the kind of body we have but also indicates how God intends for us to live. One of those purposes is the union of male and female in natural marriage. It has been this way *from the beginning*, indicating that it is God's will and purpose. To violate God's will and purpose is the definition of sin.

An immediate objection might be raised by mentioning the polygamy of the early patriarchs and some of Israel's kings. These incidents don't present the "one man, one woman" paradigm that conservatives say is God's intention. While God seems to allow polygamy for a time in Israel's history (there is no explicit command against it in Exodus, Leviticus, or Deuteronomy), it is not presented as a good thing leading to happiness. The narrative examples we see in scripture present conflict and trouble within the family that often extend for generations. When the church is being established in the New Testament era, one of the qualifications for elder is that a man must be the husband of one wife (1 Timothy 3:2, Titus 1:6). As the editors of the *ESV Study Bible* comment, "This restriction would provide a pattern that would generally lead to the abolition of polygamy in a church within a generation or two."[2]

We cannot escape the fact that the overall narrative and theology of the Bible normalize heterosexual relationships. Even within the examples of polygamy from the Old Testament, the relationship is still heterosexual in nature—a husband and multiple wives, not a husband with other men or the women amongst themselves. As Michael Brown

---

2. "Marriage and Sexual Morality," *ESV Study Bible* (Wheaton, IL: Crossway, 2008), 2,544.

comments, the Bible "presupposes heterosexuality—or, more specifically, makes clear that God created us heterosexual from the beginning."[3] Though the idea that "God made Adam and Eve, not Adam and Steve" is not all there is to be said, that statement is a faithful summary of the biblical case for natural marriage. The Bible gives us no positive examples of homosexual relationships and no teaching that applies to faithful homosexual couples. Families are expected to consist of a husband and wife and their children, if any, while adultery and sexual immorality are seen universally, throughout scripture, as sinful.

## The Destruction of Sodom and Gomorrah

*Then the Lord said, "Because the outcry against Sodom and Gomorrah is great and their sin is very grave, I will go down to see whether they have done altogether according to the outcry that has come to me. And if not, I will know."* — Genesis 18:20–21

Genesis 19 is a narrative account of God's destruction of the cities of Sodom and Gomorrah and His saving of Lot and his family. It is also the first place in scripture where we are clearly introduced to homosexual practice.[4] The account is frank in its descriptions; and even Lot, the protagonist, is

---

3. Michael L. Brown, *Can You Be Gay and Christian?* (Lake Mary, FL: FrontLine/ Charisma House Book Group, 2014), 85.

4. There is debate among commentators about whether the sin of Ham in Genesis 9:20–27 is homosexual intercourse with his father, Noah. Robert Gagnon makes a strong case that it is, but for the purposes of this study, it is more pertinent to examine Sodom and Gomorrah.

not painted in a pristine light. Because of the starkness of the descriptions and the severity of the judgment unleashed by God, Sodom and Gomorrah have been understood throughout history as a cautionary tale against the practice of homosexuality, particularly when it is accepted and becomes prevalent within a culture.

We know that Sodom is a wicked place because God has said the outcry against the city is great and "their sin is very grave," provoking God to send angels to "go down and see whether they have done altogether according to the outcry" (Genesis 18:20–21). Knowing his nephew is there, Abraham pleads with God to spare Sodom if there are as few as ten righteous people within the city.

When the angels arrive in Sodom, Lot receives them into his home after urging them not to sleep in the town square. That night, "the men of the city, the men of Sodom, both young and old, all the people to the last man, surrounded the house," demanding that the visitors be released so that the men of Sodom can have sex with Lot's visitors (Genesis 19:4–5). Lot offers his daughters to them instead, but the mob refuses. The angels rescue Lot before he can be raped and give him time to alert any relatives in town to flee from the coming destruction. The next day, God destroys the cities with fire and sulfur from heaven.

It should be plain from the text that sexual sin was so rampant that all the men of the city gathered outside Lot's house ready to sexually violate his guests. The apostle Peter sees it when he writes about Lot in 2 Peter 2:7–8:

*He [God] rescued righteous Lot, greatly distressed by the sensual conduct of the wicked (for as that righteous man lived among them day after day, he was tormenting his righteous soul over their lawless deeds that he saw and heard).*

Peter points out that their conduct was sensual and their deeds were lawless. This clearly corresponds to what we read in Genesis 19.

The apostle Jude gets even more to the point when he describes the character of their sexual immorality: "Just as Sodom and Gomorrah and the surrounding cities, which likewise indulged in sexual immorality and pursued unnatural desire, serve as an example by undergoing a punishment of eternal fire" (Jude 1:7). Furthermore, we know from Leviticus 18 that God views homosexual intercourse as an abomination in His sight. The fact that He destroyed a city full of men who were ready to commit such an act (and would have succeeded without divine intervention) should give anyone pause before seeking to affirm such debauchery.

Affirming theologians, however, are not satisfied with these explanations. Matthew Vines, for instance, claims that "the Bible never identifies same-sex behavior as the sin of Sodom, or even as *a* sin of Sodom."[5] This is quite a bold—and false—claim. Cleverly, Vines tries to base his argument on Ezekiel 16:

*Behold, this was the guilt of your sister Sodom: she and her daughters had pride, excess of food, and prosperous ease, but*

---

5. Matthew Vines, *God and the Gay Christian: The Biblical Case for Same-Sex Relationships* (New York: Convergent Books, 2014), 75.

*did not aid the poor and needy. They were haughty and did*
*an abomination before me. So I removed them, when I saw it.*
(Ezekiel 16:49–50)

The prophet does not directly name same-sex intercourse as
the sin of Sodom. He names other things instead. How do
we make sense of this while upholding biblical consistency?

The entire passage of Ezekiel 16 is spoken against
Jerusalem (Ezekiel 16:2) and is built around this imagery of
a sexually immoral prostitute (Ezekiel 16:35). The prophet
relates Jerusalem to the pagan cities of Samaria and Sodom
to symbolize the wickedness of Jerusalem's own sin (Ezekiel
16:46). The sexual sin of Sodom should have been obvious for
any Jewish reader familiar with the historic account. But what
isn't immediately apparent from the text of Genesis 19 are the
underlying causes behind the more obvious sexual rebellion
of that city: "pride, excess of food, and prosperous ease." This
is what the prophet emphasizes because it is what Jerusalem
has in common with Sodom—the people of God are on the
road to becoming Sodom.

That being said, there is still a reference to "an abomination (הָבֵעוֹת - *towʻeba*)" being committed. As theologian Robert
Gagnon argues, "The evidence indicates that the singular
*tôʻēbâ* in Ezekiel 16:50 refers to the (attempted) commission
of atrocious sexual immorality at Sodom, probably the homosexual intercourse proscribed [or outlawed] in Leviticus 18:22,
20:13."[6] Jewish readers of Ezekiel would certainly have seen
continuity among the actions described in Genesis 19, the

---

6. Robert A. J. Gagnon, *The Bible and Homosexual Practice: Texts and Hermeneutics*
(Nashville: Abingdon Press, 2001), 83–84.

command against homosexual intercourse in Leviticus, and the language of abomination in Ezekiel 16:50. In the broader context of scripture, Ezekiel 16 should be seen as both a fuller explanation of the Genesis account and a sharp warning to the people of Jerusalem that they should repent of the ways in which they might be like Sodom. It is not in opposition to or inconsistent with any other biblical statements about Sodom and Gomorrah.

Christians should not seek to minimize sin—regardless of what the sin may be. Yet this is what affirming scholars do when they want to emphasize the sins of Sodom named in Ezekiel 16. We tend to treat pride lightly, but scripture sees pride as something much darker and more depraved. It is also imbedded deeply within the desire to engage in same-sex intercourse. Robert Gagnon brings these threads together in his explanation of Ezekiel 16:

> *Pride, by definition, is the rejection of the Creator and the divinely sanctioned order of creation. Genesis 1–3, Leviticus 18:22, 20:13, and Romans 1:26–27 all suggest that same-sex intercourse was rejected on the grounds that it constituted a violation of the anatomical and procreative sexual complementarity of male and female in creation—by definition an instance of pride, supplanting of God's design in creation for sexuality in favor of one's own design.*[7]

Consider this startling visual image:

---

7. Ibid., 86n103.

*But the men reached out their hands and brought Lot into the house with them and shut the door. And they struck with blindness the men who were at the entrance of the house, both small and great, so that they wore themselves out groping for the door.* (Genesis 19:10–11)

All of the old and young men of the city have been given over to the fullness of their sinful desires. They are so committed to raping Lot and his guests that they are left groping blindly for the door. It reads like a narrative illustration of the theological description found in Romans 1, most pointedly in verse 28: "And since they did not see fit to acknowledge God, God gave them up to a debased mind to do what ought not to be done."

Genesis 19 shows a culture utterly given over to violence and sexual sin, rooted in pride, born out of excess, and negligent about caring for the needs of others. It shows us that homosexual practice is representative of the larger social degradation that comes from rejecting God. Whether the men of Sodom would identify as "homosexuals" in the sense that people now think of orientation is completely beside the point. No one can rightly read Genesis 19 and come away with a sympathetic understanding of homosexual practice. Even before the law is given, it is connected with God's impending judgment and becomes an example of wickedness for generations to come.

## The Abomination of Homosexuality

*You shall not lie with a male as with a woman; it is an abomination.* — Leviticus 18:22

Since the time it was written, Leviticus has been a definitive indictment against homosexual practice. There's a reason. The language is clear and emphatic: God hates homosexual intercourse. Leviticus 18:22 gives the command: "You shall not lie with a male as with a woman; it is an abomination." Leviticus 20:13 specifies the punishment any Israelite was due when he committed the crime in the nation of Israel: "If a man lies with a male as with a woman, both of them have committed an abomination; they shall surely be put to death; their blood is upon them."

The entire book of Leviticus stresses the distinctive holiness of the people of God in contrast to the defiling practices of the other nations surrounding them. Leviticus 18 focuses specifically on sexual morality:

*Do not make yourselves unclean by any of these things, for by all these the nations I am driving out before you have become unclean, and the land became unclean, so that I punished its iniquity, and the land vomited out its inhabitants* (Leviticus 18:24–25).

Sexual morality matters to God. This is why He gives His people the strict regulations of Leviticus 18 and why He says other peoples were being punished for their immorality.

Homosexuality is not the only form of sexual immorality discussed, but it was common enough among the pagans to warrant a direct mention by God.

Despite the clarity of these passages, some affirming theologians insist that Leviticus 18 is only prohibiting male homosexual cultic prostitution. The Rev. Joseph Adam Pearson rewrites Leviticus 18:22 this way: "You men should not dedicate your seed to any fertility god by sowing seed with a male temple cult prostitute as you would sow seed with a woman. This idolatrous practice causes you to be unclean."[8] According to Pearson's interpretation, the command has no continuing relevance to sexual ethics at all. It has a very narrow function and therefore can be easily ignored in the twenty-first century with our contemporary notions of sexual orientation and redefinition of marriage. This is blatant scriptural revision.

The existence of ancient cult prostitution has been documented, and scripture addresses it elsewhere: "None of the daughters of Israel shall be a cult prostitute, and none of the sons of Israel shall be a cult prostitute" (Deuteronomy 27:13). Deuteronomy recognizes that both men and women engaged in the practice, and it is universally outlawed. Although not all cult prostitutes engaged in homosexual intercourse, idol worship would likely have been the most common way Israelites would be exposed to and tempted by it.

Nevertheless, Leviticus 18:22 is an unqualified and absolute statement against homosexual intercourse, regardless

---

8. Joseph Adam Pearson, *Christianity and Homosexuality Reconciled: New Thinking for a New Millennium!* (Dayton, TN: Christ Evangelical Bible Institute, 2021), 155, http://christevangelicalbibleinstitute.com/ChristianityAndHomosexualityReconciled.pdf.

51

of the particulars of how it might be practiced. Sodomy may have been practiced within idol worship and temple prostitution. It may have been used as a form of subjugation in military conquest or the sexual exploitation of slaves. It may have been practiced as pederasty between grown men and young boys. It may have even been practiced between consenting adults. Yet Leviticus 18:22 is straightforward and clear. Despite affirming authors' best efforts to minimize the severity of the law, there simply is no space carved out for "committed, loving, same-sex partners" in the text. The sexual act itself is an abomination.

*Abomination* (הָבֵעוֹת – tow'ebah) means "a disgusting thing, something detestable or loathsome." Although the sins listed throughout Leviticus 18 are summarized as "abominations" in 18:24–30, homosexual practice is specifically labeled as such in both Leviticus 18:22 and 20:13. Robert Gagnon finds it noteworthy that across all of the various sins outlawed in Leviticus, "the only forbidden act to which the designation 'abomination' is specifically attached is homosexual intercourse."[9]

God's revulsion at this sin is further seen in its heavy penalty: death. "If a man lies with a male as with a woman, both of them have committed an abomination; they shall surely be put to death; their blood is upon them" (Leviticus 20:13). The fact that both parties are to be put to death implies that there is culpability on both sides ("both of them have committed an abomination"). Culpability was also implied with the sin of adultery (verse 10), incest between a man and his mother

9. Robert A. J. Gagnon, *The Bible and Homosexual Practice: Texts and Hermeneutics* (Nashville: Abingdon Press, 2001), 113.

(verse 11), and incest between a man and his daughter-in-law (verse 12). Not every sexual offense brought the same level of punishment—some incurred death, some incurred being cut off from the community, some incurred childlessness—but the penalty that some sexual offenses brought is noteworthy.

At this point in the conversation, an affirming theologian will typically say that conservative Christians do not hold every prohibition in Leviticus with equal weight. On this point we agree—as we have just seen, neither does Leviticus give equal weight to all prohibitions. Some sins are weighed and judged more severely than others. I suppose what affirming theologians are really trying to say is that Leviticus is irrelevant because evangelicals are selective in what we emphasize from the book. "If you can eat shellfish, then you shouldn't have a problem with homosexuality" is typically how this gets thrown out in conversation.

First of all, no disciple of Christ should want to minimize the law of God and presume that it is totally irrelevant today. That is not the example of Christ or the apostles. Need we be reminded that one of the favorite verses of affirming theologians is first found in Leviticus 19:18: "You shall love your neighbor as yourself."

Second, the laws of Leviticus fall into roughly three categories: ceremonial laws (governing religious practice and ceremonial cleanness), civic laws (governing how Israelites ruled their nation), and moral laws (governing the sinful behavior of people). The ceremonial laws were fulfilled in Christ as priest and sacrifice. The civic laws were uniquely given for the Hebrew people to be distinguished from other nations in their governance and social practices. Both sets of laws may still offer principles for guiding Christian ethics, but they do not bind us in the same way they did the Hebrews of old.

However, the laws that speak to morality recognize moral absolutes in the universe. The moral implications of Leviticus 18 are irrefutable because the category of sexual immorality continues to be a warning to God's people throughout the New Testament era. For example, 1 Corinthians 6:18 warns, "Flee from sexual immorality." The statements on sexuality are never rescinded or redefined later in scripture in the same way that the ceremonial laws are. In other words, Christians may eat shellfish, but they may not have homosexual intercourse.

## Uncommon Friends

*Jonathan lies slain on your high places. I am distressed for you, my brother Jonathan; very pleasant have you been to me; your love to me was extraordinary, surpassing the love of women.*
— 2 Samuel 1:26

The Bible not only speaks very negatively against homosexuality, but it also does not give us any positive depictions of homosexual behavior or homosexual relationships. This hasn't stopped certain theologians finding homoerotic undercurrents in the story of David and Jonathan—or even claiming that the men were homosexual lovers. Though this is not a mainstream position in affirming theology, it is a popular assertion in queer theology. "The story of David and Jonathan is one of those great mysteries of homoerotism in the Bible," says a student essay from the "Queer Bible Hermeneutics" class at Perkins School of Theology.[10] The idea has emotional sway with many younger people, especially those who are predisposed against traditional interpretations and eager to discover new "hidden" meanings that can be used to distance themselves from their conservative upbringings.

The record of David and Jonathan's relationship in 1 Samuel is interwoven with Saul's desperate attempts to maintain the kingdom that God had determined to remove from him (1 Samuel 15:27). Saul sinks deeper into jealousy, paranoia, and violence as the story progresses (1 Samuel 18:10–11). Contrasted with this is the Lord's blessing upon David as a mighty warrior and man of God (1 Samuel 18:14), a man also adored by the people (1 Samuel 18:5).

After David defeats Goliath, Saul takes special notice of David's valor (1 Samuel 17:57–58). Jonathan, Saul's oldest son, is also impressed with David. The text says, "The soul of Jonathan was knit to the soul of David, and Jonathan loved him as his own soul" (1 Samuel 18:1). Jonathan makes a covenant with David, giving him his own robe, armor, sword, bow, and belt as expressions of his personal loyalty and political allegiance (1 Samuel 18:3–4).

The word for *soul* (*nephesh* | נֶפֶשׁ) is also the word for "life" or "self." The word *knit* (*qashar* | קָשַׁר) carries the idea of being "bound up" or "tied." It is the same wording that appears in Judah's appeal to Joseph in Egypt about sparing the youngest son Benjamin: "Now therefore, as soon as I come to your servant my father, and the boy is not with us, then, as **his life**

10. Anonymous, "1 Samuel 18–23: The Queerness of David and Jonathan," *Queer Bible Hermeneutics* (blog), May 9, 2016, https://blog.smu.edu/ot8317/2016/05/09/1-samuel-18-23-the-queerness-of-david-and-jonathan/.

[*nephesh*] **is bound up in** [*qashar*] **the boy's life** [*nephesh*], as soon as he sees that the boy is not with us, he will die"(Genesis 44:30–31; emphasis mine). It is obviously a phrase denoting a deep love and loyalty, but it is as family, as brothers—not as erotic partners or even as we might think of romantic "soul mates." Robert Gagnon notes:

> *In effect, Jonathan is assuring David that he has hitched his fortunes to those of David, politically and emotionally. Whatever happens to David happens also to Jonathan. If David hurts, Jonathan hurts. If David rejoices, Jonathan rejoices. Consequently, if David becomes king, Jonathan has every reason to rejoice.*[11]

The men's personal bond is as brothers. However, the political aspect of Jonathan's commitment is important to see, as this is the nature of the tension between Saul and David.

Even the covenant that is forged between the two men is not the covenant of two people who just want to be together as life partners. It is a pact of survival, ensuring trust and safety—not only to the men but also to their offspring. As Jonathan says:

> *But should it please my father to do you harm, the Lord do so to Jonathan and more also if I do not disclose it to you and send you away, that you may go in safety. May the Lord be with you, as he has been with my father. If I am still alive, show me the steadfast love of the Lord, that I may not die; and do*

---

11. Robert A. J. Gagnon, *The Bible and Homosexual Practice: Texts and Hermeneutics* (Nashville: Abingdon Press, 2001), 147.

*not cut off your steadfast love from my house forever, when the Lord cuts off every one of the enemies of David from the face of the earth.* (1 Samuel 20:13–15)

This covenant is clearly between the house of David and the house of Jonathan, which Jonathan reiterates when the men are later forced to part company: "Go in peace, because we have sworn both of us in the name of the Lord, saying, 'The Lord shall be between me and you, and between my offspring and your offspring, forever.'" (1 Samuel 20:42). We see a remembrance of this covenant in David's kindness to Jonathan's son, Mephibosheth (2 Samuel 9:1–7). Their covenant was not a marriage, nor does it sound anything like one: "May the Lord take vengeance on David's enemies" (1 Samuel 20:16).

The major moment of physical affection between them is when they embrace and kiss after it becomes clear that Saul will not relent in his pursuit of David and death is imminent (1 Samuel 20:41). To a modern reader filled with Hollywood romanticism, the fact that they kiss may seem more sexualized than it would have to ancient readers. In Genesis, we find Joseph responding similarly when he reveals himself to his brothers in Egypt: "Then he fell upon his brother Benjamin's neck and wept, and Benjamin wept upon his neck. And he kissed all his brothers and wept upon them" (Genesis 45:14–15). To my knowledge, no one has ever charged Joseph with incestuous desires for his brothers.

After the death of Saul and Jonathan, we find David's lament that includes the famous lines: "I am distressed for you, my brother Jonathan; very pleasant have you been to me; your love to me was extraordinary, surpassing the love of women" (2 Samuel 1:26). This line is the proof text among those who claim that David and Jonathan were lovers. Of course, the plain reading of the entire story does not assume that sexual love is being described. As Gagnon says:

> *Jonathan's repeated display of (nonsexual) kindness to David at a time when Jonathan was in a position of power, selflessly risking his own life and certainly his own kingdom, surpassed anything David had ever known from a committed erotic relationship with a woman. No more and no less than this is the point of David's eulogy of his dear friend.*[12]

The whole eulogy is meant to honor the memory and legacy of both Saul and Jonathan. David clearly loved and respected both men. Ironically, affirming authors typically overlook or explain away the glowing statements David makes about Saul. For instance, Bruce L. Gerig comments, "In the first half, David is generous in his tribute to Saul, recalling only his good qualities; however, in the second half, David chokes up with real emotion, as he turns to speak to Jonathan."[13] Why does Gerig see the first half as "generous" (implying David is insincere about Saul) while the comments on Jonathan are where he has "real emotion"? David and Jonathan had a spiritual unity because they were both committed to the Lord's purposes. The account also makes clear that David

12. Ibid., 152–153.
13. Bruce L. Gerig, *Jonathan and David: A Love Story: A Survey of Commentary Interpretation, Textual Evidence, and Historical Background* (self-published online, 2012), 131, http://epistle.us/hbarticles/gerigbookpage.html.

loved and respected Saul and took very seriously the fact that God had anointed Saul to be king of Israel.

But let's consider briefly the "extraordinary love" Jonathan showed to David: Even though the throne would be his by birthright, Jonathan recognized, accepted, and celebrated God's intention to place David on the throne. Jonathan sought to broker peace when tensions between Saul and David mounted. Jonathan endured personal insults from his own father when Saul sensed he was protecting David. Jonathan warned his father not to sin by seeking to kill David. Jonathan did not scold David when David questioned his loyalty. Jonathan protected David from Saul by helping him to flee. Jonathan asked only that David show kindness to his offspring when the Lord destroyed David's enemies (knowing that he himself would likely be destroyed because of his loyalty to his father Saul). Surely this is extraordinary—extraordinary circumstances, certainly, but likely exceeding what many wives would realistically be willing to do for their husbands.

There simply is no evidence in the text itself to suggest that David and Jonathan were sexually—or even romantically —involved. Tom Horner was one of the first scholars to offer this suggestion, yet the historical basis for his argument is a mere assumption. Horner says:

> *David was not "homosexual" because he loved Jonathan, or Jonathan because he loved David. They were simply well-rounded men who acted fully within the standards of a society that had been dominated for two hundred years by*

*an Aegean culture [the Philistines]—a culture that accepted homosexuality.*[14]

Horner gives no proof that Philistine culture "accepted homosexuality." But his larger point is that we should combine this assumption with the interactions between David and Jonathan in the text of 1 Samuel. When we do that, Horner says, "we have every reason to believe that a homosexual relationship existed."[15]

In *Jonathan and David: A Love Story* (2012), Bruce L. Gerig gives a thorough survey of the affirming scholarship concerning the David and Jonathan story. Gerig is agreeable to the presumption of homosexuality in the story, yet in the end, he cannot speak very definitively about it. After two hundred pages of trying to debunk the historic view that David and Jonathan were simply close friends, the most definitive thing he can say in response is, "Since 'love' has many meanings, it is difficult to determine what the nature of their relationship was."[16]

In this case, the plain and obvious reading is correct. The story of David and Jonathan is not about homosexual love. Similar claims have been attempted with Ruth and Naomi as well as Jesus and the apostle John, but they are so lacking in merit that they do not even deserve comment. David and

---

14. Tom M. Horner, *Jonathan Loved David: Homosexuality in Biblical Times* (Philadelphia, PA: The Westminster Press, 1978), 24.

15. Ibid., 28.

16. Bruce L. Gerig, *Jonathan and David: A Love Story: A Survey of Commentary Interpretation, Textual Evidence, and Historical Background* (self-published online, 2012), 269, http://epistle.us/hbarticles/gerigbookpage.html.

Jonathan's friendship continues to serve as an example of sacrificial love between godly men, showing us a historical picture of Proverbs 18:24: "A man of many companions may come to ruin, but there is a friend who sticks closer than a brother."

## Dishonorable Passions

*For this reason God gave them up to dishonorable passions.*
*For their women exchanged natural relations for those that*
*are contrary to nature; and the men likewise gave up natural*
*relations with women and were consumed with passion for one*
*another, men committing shameless acts with men and receiving*
*in themselves the due penalty for their error.* — Romans
1:26–27

Romans 1 is the central text in understanding the Bible's teaching on homosexuality. The passage mentions the desire/orientation ("dishonorable passions") as well as the behavior ("committing shameless acts"), lesbianism ("for their women"), the way nature itself testifies against its propriety ("contrary to nature"), and the connection between sexual lust and rejecting God ("God gave them up"). It is a text that reads so obviously and clearly about the subject that affirming author Matthew Vines declares:

*For countless lesbian, gay, bisexual, and transgender people,*
*Romans is the book that has driven them away from their*

61

*faith and torn them from their homes and families. It's the*
*book that's sent so many down a path of despair.*[17]

After Paul's introductory comments to his readers in
Romans 1:1–15, the spiritual meat of Romans begins by
highlighting two revelations: God's righteousness and
God's wrath. In verses 16 and 17, Paul summarily says that
the righteousness of God has been revealed in the gospel
of Jesus Christ and that the way this is evident is in the
righteous living by faith (vs. 17). Rather than expounding
more on what faith is (which he will do in the following
chapters), Paul immediately starts into a detailed treatment
of the other thing revealed: the wrath of God against the
unrighteousness of mankind (vs. 18). He says this is evident
first in that a basic knowledge of God is accessible to all
people (vs. 19–20) but people reject it by not honoring
Him as God or giving Him thanks (vs. 21). He then says
that as a result of people rejecting God's natural revelation,
they become useless thinkers with darkened hearts (vs. 21).
They may claim to be wise, but they are foolish in that they
took God's glory and replaced it with images of things God
made (vs. 22).

At this point, we have quite an indictment of mankind.
But there is something more that happens. God gives them
over to the lusts of their hearts, and they embrace impurity
among themselves (vs. 24). Dishonoring God has led to dishonoring their bodies through sexual immorality. One potent
expression of this is in the embracing of homosexuality (vs.

---

17. Matthew Vines, *God and the Gay Christian: The Biblical Case for Same-Sex
Relationships* (New York: Convergent Books, 2014), 95–96.

26)—by both women and men. Even though it should be biologically obvious that men and women are fit for each other sexually, they do not even recognize that and instead are shameful in their homosexual actions and God is right to judge them (vs. 27). Since mankind rejected God, God gave their minds over to do terrible things (vs. 28). Every expression of depravity and sin can be found in mankind and a whole list of sins and wicked behaviors can be named among them (vs. 29–31). To top it off, even though they know that these actions deserve death, they not only do wickedness but also approve of others doing wickedness (vs. 32). What this does is utterly condemn mankind before God so that they are without excuse when He judges them (Romans 2:1).

Romans 1 is certainly bigger than its indictment of homosexuality. It lays the groundwork for Paul's expounding on the law, the gospel, faith, and the benefits of being united to Christ. It paints a desperate picture of mankind rejecting God and being rejected by Him. It is the state of natural man: "separated from Christ, alienated from the commonwealth of Israel and strangers to the covenants of promise, having no hope and without God in the world" (Ephesians 2:12).

Nevertheless, Paul presents homosexuality as an illustration of mankind's utter rejection of God by rejecting the natural order. Notice that Paul indicts the homosexual not for breaking the Levitical law but for embracing a sexual expression that is contrary to nature. Even without the law, Paul implies that people should be able to recognize that homosexuality is wrong because God does not make humans that way. It is destructive and degrading, and it does not lead to the procreation of new life.[18]

Indeed, Paul calls these same-sex desires "dishonorable passions" and calls homosexual intercourse a "shameless act" (ESV) or "indecent act" (NASB). As Martin Luther comments, it is only right that:

> *Those who do not have or refuse to have God in their knowledge should be plunged into the deepest and worst kind of uncleanness, because they are not only unclean of heart (which is the effect of idolatry) but also unclean of body, because those who refuse to be pure of heart cannot be pure of body.*[19]

In his estimation, homosexual desires and behavior are both a judgment and sign of idolatry of the heart.

Twentieth-century theologian Richard F. Lovelace gives a more contemporary phrasing:

---

18. Regarding the destructive practice of homosexuality, medical research has shown that many increased health risks are associated with same-sex intercourse. HIV/AIDS, hepatitis, human papillomavirus, herpes, syphilis, gonorrhea, and chlamydia are diseases that occur at a higher rate in sexually active gay men. Additionally, gay men are commonly at higher risk for eating disorders such as bulimia or anorexia nervosa. Likewise, sexually active lesbian women are at higher risks for certain gynecological cancers, STDs, and health risks related to obesity and lack of exercise. Both groups are at elevated risks of depression/anxiety, substance abuse, alcohol and tobacco addiction, and intimate partner violence.

Robert J. Winn, "Ten Things Gay Men Should Discuss with Their Healthcare Provider," *GLMA: Health Professionals Advancing LGBTQ Equality*, May 2012, http://www.glma.org/_data/n_0001/resources/live/top%2010%20forGayMen.pdf; Tonia Poteat, "Top 10 Things Lesbians Should Discuss with Their Healthcare Provider," *GLMA: Health Professionals Advancing LGBTQ Equality*, May 2012, http://www.glma.org/_data/n_0001/resources/live/Top%2010%20forlesbians.pdf.

19. Martin Luther, *Lectures on Romans*, ed. *Wilhelm Pauck* (Louisville, KY: Westminster John Knox Press, 1961), 31.

*The prevalence of disordered sexual orientation is one indication that the splendor and apparent wisdom of pagan culture are foolishness with God.... Religious concepts are not matters of indifference; they are signs and definitions of the spiritual reality which is being encountered.*[20]

So how can affirming theologians possibly dismiss Romans 1? One way is to say that Paul is describing the "excessive lust" of heterosexual men leaving their wives to seek out erotic associations with other partners, including those of the same sex. Matthew Vines says:

*Paul saw everyone as having the same basic appetite for sex. In moderation, that appetite manifested itself in heterosexual desire and behavior. But in excess, it led to same-sex desire and behavior. That is the cultural context in which Paul's original audience would have read Romans 1:26-27. Paul wasn't condemning the expression of a same-sex orientation as opposed to the expression of an opposite-sex orientation. He was condemning excess as opposed to moderation.*[21]

---

20. Richard F. Lovelace, *Homosexuality and the Church: Crisis, Conflict, Compassion* (Old Tappan, NJ: Fleming H. Revell, 1978), 69. In my opinion, Lovelace is too generous toward the spiritual sincerity of avowed and practicing "homosexual Christians" in evangelical denominations and toward the emergence of "homophile religion" (as he puts it). This is why an unhelpful part of his statement has been excised from the quotation above. Overall, Lovelace does hold a proper biblical understanding of homosexuality but softens the application to his own day, likely because the question of ordaining homosexual pastors in the United Presbyterian Church was a current debate splitting his own denomination in the late 1970s.

21. Matthew Vines, *God and the Gay Christian: The Biblical Case for Same-Sex Relationships* (New York: Convergent Books, 2014), 105.

It should be obvious that excessive lust is condemned because all lust is condemned. But the text of Romans 1:26–27 is showing that homosexuality is beyond the bounds of normal relations and is excessive *in itself*. Nowhere in this text is Paul carving out the possibility of "the expression of a same-sex orientation" in the way that Vines conceives it.

The strongest argument affirming theologians can muster is that Paul is talking exclusively about same-sex relations within an idolatrous context. Therefore, they say, he isn't really concerned with other forms of same-sex relations, such as committed partnerships. One affirming author succinctly summarized his understanding of Paul like this: "Leaving your wife/husband to have same-gender sex in idol worship is wrong."[22] This interpretation sounds agreeable only if someone has already rejected or revised the condemnation of homosexual intercourse in Leviticus 18 and 20.

Romans 1 does recognize the depth of idolatry in natural man, but the language Paul uses against homosexuality goes beyond sex in idol worship. "Contrary to nature" says nothing about idolatry. Romans 1:26–27 does not even hint at idolatry. When Paul speaks elsewhere about the sanctity of marriage, he alludes to Genesis 2, which describes a man and woman fit for each other and becoming one flesh. Paul's theology is consistent; the revisionist's is not. According to the revisionist's faulty logic, we might as well argue that adultery is permissible so long as it isn't within the context of idol worship, despite the fact that scripture teaches that adultery is wrong

---

22. John Elliott Lein, "Same-Sex Marriage and Homosexuality: What about the Bible?" Gay Marriage and the Bible, 2015, http://www.gaymarriageandthebible.com/.

regardless of whether physical idol worship is involved or not.

Furthermore, affirming theologians completely miss that Paul's view of idolatry goes deeper than the physical acts of bowing down or offering sacrifices. Notice that in Ephesians 5:5, Paul calls *covetousness* idolatry. "For you may be sure of this, that everyone who is sexually immoral or impure, or who is covetous (that is, an idolater), has no inheritance in the kingdom of Christ and God." How can Paul say this? He does not mean that the only people who are considered sexually immoral or covetous are those practicing physical idol worship. No, his linking of *sexual immorality* with *covetousness* assumes that there is a wrongful desire undergirding anything that happens physically. This could happen in a cultic temple or in someone's home or anywhere else. This desire for something that God has not ordained or allowed is idolatrous in itself. And the person whose life is marked by sexual immorality, impurity, and covetousness is an idolater who will not inherit the kingdom of God.

Every attempt to reframe Paul's clear language in Romans 1 refuses to understand the context of Paul himself. Where would Paul—"Hebrew of Hebrews" that he was—have built his understanding of sexual ethics? Genesis and Leviticus. The practitioners of Judaism from the giving of the law to Paul's day would never have understood there to be a "good version" of homosexual behavior, and it's fair to say that neither Paul nor his readers would have found that to be a plausible reading of Romans. Homosexual historians like Louis Crompton find it "strained and unhistorical" to make Paul somehow seem pro-gay: "Nowhere does Paul or any other Jewish writer of this period imply the least acceptance of same-sex relations under any circumstance."[23]

Many affirming theologians make it sound as if humans began to think deeply about sexuality only in the nineteenth and twentieth centuries. This is why many revisionists simply say that Paul was innocently ignorant—he didn't express things in the best way because he didn't have the vocabulary or framework to do so. But classical scholars, such as N.T. Wright, believe these arguments are overstated. Wright explains:

> *As a classicist, I have to say that when I read Plato's Symposium, or when I read the accounts from the early Roman empire of the practice of homosexuality, then it seems to me they knew just as much about it as we do. In particular, a point which is often missed, they knew a great deal about what people today would regard as longer-term, reasonably stable relations between two people of the same gender. This is not a modern invention, it's already there in Plato.*[24]

Indeed, many pro-LGBT scholars have researched homosexuality, bisexuality, and lesbianism in the cultures of classical Greece and Rome and have found a surprisingly diverse record of sexual expression within those cultures—including many concepts and behaviors that sound

---

23. Louis Crompton, *Homosexuality and Civilization*. (Cambridge, MA: Harvard University Press, 2003), 114.

24. John L. Allen, Jr., "Interview with Anglican Bishop N.T. Wright of Durham, England," *National Catholic Reporter*, May 21, 2004, http://www.nationalcatholicreporter.org/word/wright.htm.

shockingly contemporary. It is fair to assume that Paul was not nearly so ignorant of these things as many affirming theologians have claimed.

Apart from being brazenly arrogant, this revisionist thinking is an assault on the authority of the scripture and its inspiration by the Holy Spirit—God's ability to truthfully communicate His words through human agents. Why should anyone take the scripture seriously if an all-knowing God can't even set the record straight on sexuality two thousand years ahead of time? If the church has gotten homosexuality wrong from the beginning, then why didn't God do anything to clarify it when He was the one writing scripture? This is where many affirming theologians end up—questioning God's character as revealed in scripture.

The entire revisionist project is one that approaches scripture suspiciously—seeking to wed worldly thinking with the text of the Bible. As long as there are affirming theologians who want to claim that the Bible is authoritative, there will be attempts to get out from underneath the clear implications of Romans 1:26–27. This is why many of these revisionists end up rejecting biblical authority at some point. It's too hard to remain consistent. As Kevin DeYoung put it:

*There is no positive case for homosexual practice in the Bible and no historical background that will allow us to set aside what has been the plain reading of scripture for twenty centuries. The only way to think the Bible is talking about every other kind of homosexuality except the kind we want to affirm is to be less than honest with the texts or less than honest with ourselves.*[25]

## Effeminate and Homosexuals

*Or do you not know that the unrighteous will not inherit the kingdom of God? Do not be deceived; neither fornicators, nor idolaters, nor adulterers,* **nor effeminate**, **nor homosexuals**, *nor thieves, nor the covetous, nor drunkards, nor revilers, nor swindlers, will inherit the kingdom of God. And such were some of you. But you were washed, you were sanctified, you were justified in the name of the Lord Jesus Christ and by the Spirit of our God.* —1 Corinthians 6:9–11 (NASB; emphasis mine)

*But we know that the Law is good, if one uses it lawfully, realizing the fact that law is not made for a righteous person, but for those who are lawless and rebellious, for the ungodly and sinners, for the unholy and profane, for those who kill their fathers or mothers, for murderers and immoral men* **and homosexuals** *and kidnappers and liars and perjurers, and whatever else is contrary to sound teaching, according to the glorious gospel of the blessed God, with which I have been entrusted.* — 1 Timothy 1:8–11 (NASB; emphasis mine)

---

25. Kevin DeYoung, *What Does the Bible Really Teach about Homosexuality?* (Wheaton, IL: Crossway, 2015), 87.

In Paul's letters of 1 Corinthians and 1 Timothy, there are two Greek words that are of interest to anyone studying the Bible's teaching on homosexuality: *malakoi* (μαλακός translated in the NASB as "effeminate" in 1 Corinthians 6:9) and *arsenokoitai* (ἀρσενοκοίτης translated in the NASB as "homosexuals" in 1 Corinthians 6:9 and 1 Timothy 1:10). These words are not extremely common in ancient literature, yet Paul uses them in these two separate lists of unrighteous people.

The mentions of homosexuality in these epistles, while different in character from those in Leviticus and Romans, are morally consistent with the other biblical passages. First Corinthians 6:9–11 gives a list of wicked ways of living that will keep someone barred from God's kingdom. First Timothy 1:8–11 gives a list of rebellious people who are part of the very reason why God gave His law. These lists include both general and specific sins, and homosexuality is one sinful way of living in a list of many. Nevertheless, we cannot escape these two words that show up in these verses—nor should we ignore them.

*Arsenokoitai* ("homosexuals") literally means "man-bedders." It is a word that some scholars believe was coined by the Apostle Paul in these epistles because it is the first place that we find the word in the surviving literature of antiquity. The word is clearly a construction of the Greek words *arsēn* (for "male") and *koitē* (for "bed" or "to lie"). Paul may or may not have coined the term *arsenokoitai*, but the root words seem to pull directly from the language of Leviticus 18:22: "And you shall not lie with a male [*arsēn*] as lying [*koitē*] with a woman; that is a detestable thing" (Lexham English

Bible). The stark make-up of the word testifies to the clarity of its meaning. Even Matthew Vines admits that if *arsenokoitai* is rooted in the Greek wording of Leviticus, Paul "*was likely using the word to condemn some form of same-sex behavior.*"[26] Vines wants to mix the truth with his own speculation, however, implying that whatever Paul is saying, he is certainly not condemning the kind of homosexual behavior Matthew Vines wants to affirm!

Is the word *homosexuals* an accurate translation of *arsenokoitai*? Many revisionists like to tell conservatives that *homosexuals* never appeared in the Bible before 1946—alluding to the fact that the Revised Standard Version (RSV) was the first English Bible to make that translation choice. This historical detail is irrelevant as to the meaning of *arsenokoitai*, however. The term refers to men who bed other men. As the term *homosexual* replaced *sodomite* in common use, the later translators utilized it and have continued to do so going forward. It is noted that Paul is not using the word *arsenokoitai* to describe a "homosexual orientation" in the way many people think of it today. Nevertheless, while modern psychology may want to pack additional meanings into the word *homosexual*, it should be uncontroversial to use *homosexual* to describe a person who engages in same-sex intercourse. The biblical teaching on homosexuality is not derived from this one word; rather, the biblical teaching informs our understanding of it.

The other word to understand is *malakoi* ("effeminate"). *Malakoi* literally means "soft," although it can be understood

---

26. Matthew Vines, *God and the Gay Christian: The Biblical Case for Same-Sex Relationships* (New York: Convergent Books, 2014), 123.

as "luxurious," "effeminate," or the passive partner in male homosexual intercourse, depending on the context. Affirming theologians frequently cast doubt on our ability to understand the word with any degree of clarity. However, Robert Gagnon gives a thorough treatment of the context and use of the word both in scripture and in other ancient Greek sources. Gagnon says, "In my own reading, the meaning of *malakoi* in 1 Corinthians 6:9 probably lies somewhere in between 'only prostituting passive homosexuals' and 'effeminate heterosexual and homosexual males.'"[27] He sees the placement of *malakoi* within the list in 1 Corinthians 6 as significant in charging the meaning with sexual undertones—fornicators, idolaters, adulterers, *malakoi*, homosexuals/man-bedders.

Gagnon also believes there is a more general sense of "playing the woman" likely alluded to by the word. This comes from Philo, a first-century Jewish author, who used *malakoi* to describe men "who cultivate feminine features . . . men who braid their hair and who use makeup and excessive perfume in an effort to please their male lovers."[28] Gagnon's final verdict is that "*malakoi* should be understood as the passive partners in homosexual intercourse, the most egregious case of which are those who intentionally engage in a process of feminization to erase further their masculine appearance and manner."[29]

Interpreters have known this for centuries, yet, unsurprisingly, revisionists reject this meaning of *malakoi*. Some prefer a very narrow meaning, such as "effeminate call-boys"

---

27. Robert A. J. Gagnon, *The Bible and Homosexual Practice: Texts and Hermeneutics* (Nashville: Abingdon Press, 2001), 307–308.

28. Ibid., 308.

29. Ibid., 312.

(young male prostitutes), while others put together a very broad list of potential meanings, including anything from soft clothes to laziness to cowardice to an overactive sex life or, as Matthew Vines says, "an entire disposition toward immoderation."[30] This is all an attempt to render the word meaningless. But its pairing with *arsenokoitai* in the text leaves very little mystery as to how it should be understood, and the translation "effeminate" seems to capture the meaning well.

The warning in 1 Corinthians 6:9–10 is a loving reminder not to be deceived: "The unrighteous will not inherit the kingdom of God." Yet the warning blossoms into a beautiful testimony of God's mercy in verse 11: "And such were some of you. But you were washed, you were sanctified, you were justified in the name of the Lord Jesus Christ and by the Spirit of our God." This is notable. Paul is writing to people who had once been deeply committed to sinful behavior— including homosexuality and effeminacy—who are now submitting themselves to the Lord and growing in godliness to the point where those things no longer define their lives. Those sins have been laid aside.

This comes as a rebuke to anyone who claims their homosexuality is innate and immutable, which is why even "gay celibate Christians" resist this reading of 1 Corinthians 6:11. They want to maintain that their psychological state as "gay" or "nonstraight" is their true self and that their same-sex attraction will always remain unchanged. Many "gay celibate Christians" have cultivated their own effeminate dress, hair style, mannerisms, and speech, replacing the expression of

---

30. Matthew Vines, *God and the Gay Christian: The Biblical Case for Same-Sex Relationships* (New York: Convergent Books, 2014), 122.

their God-given sex with queer self-expression. Sadly, those who do this frequently end up turning away from biblical truth, embracing affirming or queer theology that allows them to seek out gay relationships. Rather than submitting their temptations to the Lord and seeking the renewal of the mind by the Word, they are defiled and defined by their own desires and eventually mastered by them. But the love of God in the hearts of sincere followers is manifested in departure from sinful behavior in word, thought, and deed. There is freedom in the promise "such were some of you." This is the great hope we have in overcoming sin in this life. Christians are of those who once *were*.

Paul's words remain an encouragement to any sincere Christian who has seen their sinful habits and ways of thinking overcome by God's grace. Robert Gagnon concludes his exegesis of 1 Corinthians 6:9–11 with this encouraging reminder:

> *God both empowers believers by means of the Spirit, and motivates them through God's unprecedented accomplishment of redemption in Christ and the hope of a magnificent salvation yet to be revealed. The God who once manifested wrath against those who turned to idols by handing them over to their shameful passions has now handed them over to the life-giving, transformative power of the Spirit of Christ. The former manner of life bore fruit that would lead to death; the new manner of life bears fruit that leads to eternal life.*[31]

---

31. Robert A. J. Gagnon, *The Bible and Homosexual Practice: Texts and Hermeneutics* (Nashville: Abingdon Press, 2001), 338.

The need to warn has never been greater, as we remind souls of the enormous gain of eternal life for the repentant and the enormous loss of eternal death for those who reject Christ's love by embracing sin.

## Jesus and Sexual Ethics

*Have you not read that he who created them from the beginning made them male and female, and said, "Therefore a man shall leave his father and his mother and hold fast to his wife, and the two shall become one flesh"?* — Matthew 19:4–5

"Homosexuality was well known in the ancient world, well before Christ was born and Jesus never said a word about homosexuality."[32] So says former President Jimmy Carter. Many Christians have heard a similar statement before, implying that if Jesus didn't say anything about homosexuality directly, then He doesn't have an opinion about it. Affirming theologians fill in the silence with affirmation and use it to shut down Christians in the LGBT debate. Everyone wants Jesus on their side. But what did Jesus actually believe about sexuality?

Christians should recognize that on its face, President Carter's statement is factual. Jesus did not specifically reference homosexuality in any of His statements recorded for us in the four gospels. But President Carter's statement

---

32. "President Jimmy Carter Authors New Bible Book, Answers Hard Biblical Questions," HuffPost, March 19, 2012, https://www.huffpost.com/entry/president-jimmy-carter-bible-book_n_1349570.

is misleading because what is recorded for us in the gospels is Jesus' view of the law, creation, marriage, divorce, and sexual morality—all of which are consistent with the rest of scripture that we have seen thus far.

Before we examine Jesus' sexual ethics, we must first acknowledge that Jesus understood the Old Testament scriptures to be fully true and authoritative. He taught that the scriptures are inspired by God Himself (Matthew 22:43), that they would not pass away until all was fulfilled (Matthew 5:17–18), that they are infallible (John 10:35), that they have final authority (Matthew 4:4, 7, 10), that they are historically reliable (Matthew 12:40; 24:37), that they are wholly true (John 17:17; Matthew 22:29), that they can be clearly understood (Luke 24:25), and that they are fully sufficient to hold mankind accountable for our thoughts and actions in this life (Luke 16:31). Whatever we say about Jesus' views on anything should be consistent with the overall biblical teaching since Jesus and the Father are one (John 10:30).

Jesus' understanding of marriage is not unique to Himself but is grounded in Genesis 2. For instance, in Matthew 19, when Jesus is questioned about the lawfulness of divorce, He grounds His response in Genesis 2:24, further commenting, "So they are no longer two but one flesh. What therefore God has joined together, let not man separate" (Matthew 19:6). This response indicates that Jesus not only takes the Genesis account of creation literally, but He also takes it as instructive to inform Christian ethics. He also holds up natural marriage as normative and expected by linking it to God's created order in biology:

*Have you not read that he who created them from the beginning made them male and female, and said, "Therefore a man shall leave his father and his mother and hold fast to his wife, and the two shall become one flesh"?* (Matthew 19:4–5).

Jesus holds the "one flesh" sexual bond of husband and wife in such high regard that it is reflected in His particularly strong view of divorce and remarriage:

*It was also said, "Whoever divorces his wife, let him give her a certificate of divorce." But I say to you that everyone who divorces his wife, except on the ground of sexual immorality, makes her commit adultery, and whoever marries a divorced woman commits adultery.* (Matthew 5:31–32)

In this statement, sexual immorality is the only valid grounds for divorce, and without those grounds, adultery is committed when either party is remarried.

The word for "sexual immorality" is used again by Jesus in Mark 7:21 when He says, "For from within, out of the heart of man, come evil thoughts, sexual immorality, theft, murder, adultery, coveting, wickedness, deceit, sensuality, envy, slander, pride, foolishness." The Greek word for "sexual immorality" is *porneia* (πορνεία), which refers to illicit sexual intercourse—meaning any sexual behavior that would have been forbidden by the Torah.

Considering that Christ loved, honored, and perfectly understood the law of God, we have no reason to think He would make any exception to the sexual law without noting it. We see in the same passage in Mark that Jesus' statement did that very thing with the food laws:

*And he said to them, "Then are you also without understanding? Do you not see that whatever goes into a person from outside cannot defile him, since it enters not his heart but his stomach, and is expelled?" (Thus he declared all foods clean.)* (Mark 7:18–19).

Yet Christ's statement, while dismissing the food laws, still holds to the moral laws, including those regarding sexuality.

Finally, in that famous statement from the Sermon on the Mount, Jesus acknowledges that sin goes deeper than the letter of the law: "You have heard that it was said, 'You shall not commit adultery.' But I say to you that everyone who looks at a woman with lustful intent has already committed adultery with her in his heart" (Matthew 5:27–28). This is not a minimizing of sexual sin, nor is it a revision of the Levitical law. As Robert Gagnon observes:

*The impression one gets from Matthew 5:27–32 is that Jesus took sexual sin very seriously—in some respects more seriously than the prevailing culture in first-century Palestine. He regarded all sexual activity (thoughts and deeds) outside of lifelong marriage to one person of the opposite sex as capable of jeopardizing one's entrance into the kingdom of God. In our own cultural context, Jesus' views on sex represent on the whole a staunchly conservative position.*[33]

---

33. Robert A. J. Gagnon, *The Bible and Homosexual Practice: Texts and Hermeneutics* (Nashville: Abingdon Press, 2001), 209.

Jesus may not have said anything directly about homosexuality, but it is impossible to stay true to the teaching of Jesus and embrace homosexuality as holy, good, or normal. Michael Brown summarizes it well when he says, "It is unconscionable to imagine that Jesus would sanction male-male or female-female unions, since, among other things, they fundamentally violate God's design and intent 'from the beginning.'"[34]

In fact, those who should be most troubled by Jesus' silence on homosexuality are those in the affirming camp. If Jesus truly affirms homosexual relationships, He could have set a precedent for Christian teaching forever going forward, removing the stigma from homosexual intercourse and affirming the committed relationships of same-sex partners. Yet He never did. In light of that far more damning silence, we can either submit ourselves to what He taught or find ourselves counted as "workers of lawlessness" (Matthew 7:23).

## Eunuchs and the Kingdom of Heaven

*For there are eunuchs who have been so from birth, and there are eunuchs who have been made eunuchs by men, and there are eunuchs who have made themselves eunuchs for the sake of the kingdom of heaven. Let the one who is able to receive this receive it.* — Matthew 19:12

One topic that has gained increased interest among gay affirming authors and queer theorists over the years is the

34. Michael L. Brown, *Can You Be Gay and Christian?* (Lake Mary, FL: FrontLine/ Charisma House Book Group, 2014), 133.

descriptions of eunuchs found in antiquity. The obvious reason for this is that contemporary minds that are set on approving homosexuality want to find some way of highlighting its perdurance in society throughout history. Eunuchs have garnered much speculation because they sometimes seem to inhabit an androgynous "third sex" category, especially among some of the most decadent of Roman emperors.[35] This idea gets linked to Christ's words in Matthew 19:12—especially the thought of a "born eunuch"—and then the debate emerges from there, intended to baffle Christians who are likely unfamiliar with eunuchs altogether. Therefore, some context is necessary before we can address the reframing of Christ's words by affirming scholars.

In basic definition, a *eunuch* was a man who was castrated in order to serve in an official capacity to a ruler. This castration may have included just the eunuch's testicles or both the testicles and penis in total, although a total castration was more dangerous and could result in death from blood loss. If the castration occurred before puberty, the overall physical development, voice, and appearance of the man would be impacted. Though different ancient civilizations utilized and thought of eunuchs in different ways, castration has been universally considered the defining mark of a eunuch.[36] In the Bible, eunuchs are mentioned several times in the Old Testament, and their references are almost exclusively

---

35. For example, after his wife Poppaea Sabina died, Roman Emperor Nero married a slave boy named Sporus. Nero castrated the boy and tried to "remake" him into a woman, having him dress up in woman's clothes, take on the empress's name, and appear as the emperor's wife in public.

36. Vern L. Bullough, "Eunuchs in History and Society," *Eunuchs in Antiquity and Beyond*, ed. Shaun Tougher (Swansea, Wales: The Classical Press of Wales, 2002), 1.

surrounding court officials, such as in Daniel 1:7 ("And the chief of the eunuchs gave them names…") and Esther 1:10 ("he commanded . . . the seven eunuchs who served in the presence of King Ahasuerus").

The Hebrew word *saris* (סָרִיס) appears 38 times in the original texts of the Old Testament and can mean "eunuch" or, more generally, "an official or officer." The word is translated different ways depending on the context. In the cases above in Esther and Daniel, the word is translated *eunuch* because of the historical evidence that Babylon and Persia utilized castrated eunuchs in their courts—particularly to be the overseers of a king's harem, as in the case of Hegai, "the king's eunuch, who is in charge of the women" (Esther 2:3). In the case of Samuel's warning about Israel establishing a king in 1 Samuel 8:15 ("He will take the tenth of your grain and of your vineyards and give it to his officers [*saris*] and to his servants."), the word is translated *officers* because the Hebrews did not practice castration, so any future *saris* would be *officers* rather than *eunuchs*. Likewise, in the case of Potiphar in Genesis 37:36 ("Potiphar, an officer [*saris*] of Pharaoh, the captain of the guard."), his role is translated as *officer* since he is married (Genesis 39:7), which makes it highly unlikely that he would have been castrated.[37]

There is no evidence that the Hebrew people ever practiced castration—in fact, Judaism consistently outlawed the practice for both humans and animals throughout its

---

37. For a careful breakdown of each use of *saris* across the Old Testament and whether they may be referring to a true eunuch or an officer, see F. P. Retief, J.F.G. Cilliers, and S.P.J.K. Riekert, "Eunuchs in the Bible," *Acta Theologica* 26, no. 2 (2006): Supplementum 7, https://doi.org/10.4314/actat.v26i2.52578.

history.[38] The Levitical law never gave castration as a punishment for crimes. Those who had "crushed testicles" were not allowed to serve as priests (Leviticus 21:20), and those who had been castrated or who otherwise had mutilated genitals were barred from the assembly of the Lord (Deuteronomy 23:1). Additionally, animals that had been castrated were not allowed to be offered as a sacrifice (Leviticus 22:24). "Since there is a blemish in them, because of their mutilation, they will not be accepted for you" (Leviticus 22:25).

The idea of rejecting "blemishes"—as a reflection of God's supreme holiness and perfection—probably gives the best indication for why a eunuch would have been excluded from the assembly. However, in Isaiah 56:1–8, there is a prophecy concerning the New Covenant wherein the Lord blesses the God-fearing eunuch, saying, "I will give in my house and within my walls a monument and a name better than sons and daughters; I will give them an everlasting name that shall not be cut off" (Isaiah 56:5). This is not evidence that eunuchs were a common part of Israel's society but is part of God's intention to include the Gentiles in His kingdom, thereby making His temple "a house of prayer for all peoples" (Isaiah 56:7), where even the eunuch—formerly an outsider by the law—is given a place of honor. The language regarding eunuchs in Isaiah 56 indicates that however eunuchs may be considered in other ancient cultures, the Hebrew people understood them to be people without families, with their way of establishing a generational name having been literally "cut off."

---

38. "Castration," *Jewish Virtual Library* (accessed November 19, 2020), https://www.jewishvirtuallibrary.org/castration-jewish-virtual-library.

So when we arrive at Christ's words in Matthew 19:12, we must carry this Jewish context into His statements regarding eunuchs. We must also hold the context of the immediate passage at the forefront. In this we recognize that Jesus is responding to the disciples' shock at His strong teaching against divorce and remarriage. "The disciples said to him, 'If such is the case of a man with his wife, it is better not to marry.'" (Matthew 19:10). In response to this, Jesus says:

> *Not everyone can receive this saying, but only those to whom it is given. For there are eunuchs who have been so from birth, and there are eunuchs who have been made eunuchs by men, and there are eunuchs who have made themselves eunuchs for the sake of the kingdom of heaven. Let the one who is able to receive this receive it.* (Matthew 19:11–12)

The whole point of Christ's statement is to highlight those who are not going to be married—there are some who are born with injury or defect, some who are mutilated by others, and some who are otherwise bodily whole but forego marriage and family for the sake of spreading the gospel. Though this might be the most conclusive teaching on eunuchs in the entire Bible, its purpose is not actually to teach us about new categories of eunuchs. It is to stress that either a husband and wife are to be committed to each other in marriage or a person must be committed to celibacy. A person who can receive the lifelong charge of celibacy should recognize that it is providentially given; a person who cannot receive that charge would, therefore, seek to be committed in natural marriage for the rest of their lives.

This has been the unquestioned interpretation of this passage for centuries. It was even the position held by the early church father Origen, who is rumored to have castrated himself as a young adult. Origen said this about Matthew 19:12:

> But one must not give credence to those who do not understand the intention of the holy letters concerning these things. For if "self-control" was mentioned among the fruits "of the Spirit" with love, and joy, long-suffering, and the rest (Galatians 5:22–23), one must certainly produce the fruit of self-control, and one must preserve [intact] the male body which was given by God, rather than ever dare to do some other thing, in order that one may not transgress what is said with benefit even according to a literal reading: "You will not ruin the appearance of your beard." (Leviticus 19:27)[39]

Even with that interpretive framework, we might still wonder about the exact meaning of the "born eunuch" in Matthew 19. The Greek word *eunouchos* (εὐνοῦχος) carries the same inferences as the Hebrew word—a castrated man in office.[40] However, it does seem evident that in Greek and Roman cultures by this point in history, *eunuchs* had become more of a figurative term for castrated personal slaves rather than a description of a government role. Some people at this

---

39. Origen of Alexandria, *Origen of Alexandria, Commentary on the Gospel according to Matthew: Book 15*, trans. Justin M. Gohl (2019), 9, https://www.academia.edu/31581897/Origen_of_Alexandrias_Commentary_on_Matthew_Book_15_An_English_Translation_Revised_2019_.

40. *Thayer's Greek Lexicon*, Electronic Database, "Lexicon: Strong's G2135 – eunouchos." Biblesoft Inc.

time derisively referred to impotent men as a kind of eunuch, even though they may not have been physically castrated. If impotence is being more broadly included by Christ in His statement, it seems to be an impotence that did not develop later in life but something congenital and therefore making a man undesirable as a husband.

It is within this aspect of implied impotence that some affirming authors have really homed in, taking this to be a validation of a person who is born gay (and therefore impotent with women and unable to procreate). As John J. McNeill claims in his 1976 book *The Church and the Homosexual*, the "born eunuch" in Matthew 19 is "the closest description we have in the Bible of what we understand today as a homosexual."[41] Of course, this is a deeply metaphorical reading not only of Christ's words but also of the very concept of eunuchs. Therefore, according to McNeill's reasoning, Jesus' use of "the term *eunuch* applies to all those who are sexually different and who, for whatever reason, do not procreate."[42] McNeill has no historical or biblical basis for claiming this except that he simply wants it to be so.

Similarly, semantic scholar J. David Hester argued that because there were historical examples of Greco-Roman eunuchs who were not celibate or chaste, the very mention of eunuchs by Jesus "confronts us and demands that we face up to and reassess the assumptions we have about the

---

41. John T. McNeill, *The Church and the Homosexual*, 4th ed. (Boston, MA: Beacon Press, 1993), 64–65.

42. John T. McNeill, *Taking a Chance on God: Liberating Theology for Gays, Lesbians, and Their Lovers, Families, and Friends* (Boston, MA: Beacon Press, 1988), 155.

sanctity of heterosexist ideology."[43] But as we have already seen, Jesus' sexual ethics would have been right in line with those specified in the Torah—so Jesus' use of the eunuch as an illustration of devotion to God cannot be an affirmation of deviant sexual expression. Robert Gagnon likewise notes that even if someone is homosexually inclined, "inherent in the concept of 'eunuchs for the kingdom of heaven' is the requirement of giving up all sexual activity. One can only conclude that the saying gives absolutely no support for same-sex intercourse."[44]

J. David Hester's take is essentially a queer reading, where original context and authorial intent are ignored in favor of something that intentionally subverts traditional interpretation. He admits as much when he says, "In what follows, I will problematize the 'celibate' eunuch by reference to ancient historical gender systems that undermine the traditional masculinist and heterosexist reading of this verse."[45] Hester's reading is decidedly political, which is why he concludes his paper by saying, "The eunuch confronts us and demands that we face up to and reassess the assumptions we have about the sanctity of heterosexist ideology."[46]

There is much contradictory and unclear material in ancient Greece and Rome regarding eunuchs, and classical

---

43. J. David Hester, "Eunuchs and the Postgender Jesus: Matthew 19:12 and Transgressive Sexuality," *Journal for the Study of the New Testament* 28, no. 1 (September 2005): 40, https://doi.org/10.1177%2F0142064X05057772.

44. Robert A. J. Gagnon, *The Bible and Homosexual Practice: Texts and Hermeneutics* (Nashville: Abingdon Press, 2001), 118.

45. J. David Hester, "Eunuchs and the Postgender Jesus: Matthew 19:12 and Transgressive Sexuality" *Journal for the Study of the New Testament* 28, no. 1 (September 2005): 15, https://doi.org/10.1177%2F0142064X05057772.

46. Ibid., 40.

scholars have struggled to understand how to interpret it all. Needless to say, it should not offer a legitimate challenge to the traditional Christian understanding of Matthew 19:12 since Christ's words stand outside of the vile Roman satire and poetry that is shaping the thinking of scholars like J. David Hester. Nevertheless, as queer theorists continue to read into antiquity to find examples of "sexual minorities" and "gender nonconforming" individuals, expect the citation of eunuchs as proof against the biblical worldview to increase.

## What's the Problem?

*Though they know God's righteous decree that those who practice such things deserve to die, they not only do them but give approval to those who practice them.* — Romans 1:32

This chapter serves only as an introduction and summary of what the Bible teaches on sexuality. More detail could be given to answer every objection more thoroughly, and there are a number of books out there that do so.[47] But the truth is that affirming theologians do not want to hear sound answers to their objections. They have a prior commitment to affirming homosexuality that takes precedence over any plain reading of scriptural text or accurate assessment of Christian theology. Instead, they find themselves in a position of needing to cast doubt on the basic meaning of biblical passages. *"Did God actually say?"* In the minds of

---

47. Robert A. J. Gagnon, *The Bible and Homosexual Practice* (Nashville: Abingdon Press, 2001) gives the fullest, most detailed scholarly defense.

activists and LGBT defenders, the faster the Bible can be removed from the discussion of homosexuality, the better. Even many "gay Christians" want to remove the Bible from the discussion because they know it hurts their cause.

Why does it matter that the Bible calls homosexuality a sin? God's law is a reflection of His character and the central means He uses to bring sinners to repentance. If we were to reconfigure or redefine how the Bible speaks against lying, for instance, we would be altering one of the ways God's law is intended to convict sinners of sin. Liars would suddenly find themselves absolved of wrongdoing and no longer needy of God's gracious forgiveness in Christ because maybe they aren't truly liars after all. It is a frightful thing to alter not only God's words but also the implications that He has set on them.

Sadly, many professing Christians have already made subtle compromises that allow for divorce and remarriage, pornography use, adultery, sexual abuse, and sex outside of marriage. They might still call those things sinful in general but not in their particular situation or the situation of someone they refuse to disparage. Most likely, this compromise didn't begin with an outright rejection of scripture but a nuanced view of scripture's implications. It began with justifying a friend or not wanting to be seen as harsh. These things start small. Words matter, and God's words matter more than any others. If we adjust them or what they are intended to communicate to appease the hearts of sinful people, we should not be surprised when scripture is adapted to justify all kinds of unrighteousness. If we treat the Bible as if it lacks power to save and authority to convict, we should not be surprised when it is no longer preached with power or received with eagerness.

Activists make much of the Bible's teaching about love, but they completely redefine it. "Love is love" is a popular LGBT slogan that expresses sentimental nonsense. Love is not self-evident. It is not an experience or emotion we define but something God has already defined for us. In 1 Corinthians 13, one of the most famous passages on love in any literature, Paul lays out a list of attitudes and responses that demonstrate what biblical love looks like. It is patient and kind; it is not proud. It does not insist on its own way. But embedded within a list of attributes most people appreciate is a biblical ideal often forgotten in this debate. "Love does not rejoice at wrongdoing, but rejoices with the truth" (1 Corinthians 13:6).

It is not loving to call something *good* and *right* that the Bible labels an "abomination," "dishonorable passion," or "shameless act." This goes for any sin, not just homosexuality. Further, if someone says they love God, this is how we measure the validity of that claim (1 John 1:6). Sin separates us from God and is the reason Christ came. But if we reject Christ by declaring ourselves righteous, then there is no sacrifice for us because Christ declared that we must turn away from our sin (Hebrews 10:26–27). We can have no hope of peace with God or life everlasting if we reject the words of Christ: "Repent, for the kingdom of heaven is at hand" (Matthew 4:17).

The warnings of scripture are there for a reason. If we do not heed them, then we make God our enemy. If we do this, we will have to answer to Him for how we have twisted

His clear words to us and led others astray by our dangerous affirmations.

# CHAPTER 3

# RETHINKING THE CHURCH

There is a general perception that LGBT people hate religion. While there are plenty of spiteful atheists in the gay community, there are also many who participate in religious services of all kinds and say that their faith is an important part of their life. According to a 2015 Pew Research study, as many as 48% of lesbian, gay, or bisexual people identify generally as Christian, while 13% consider themselves evangelicals.[1] Nevertheless, Christianity is not perceived as friendly toward LGBT people. Another study found that 73% of LGBT people consider evangelical churches generally unfriendly toward them.[2]

Since nearly half of LGBT people identify as Christian in some way, this has given rise to "gay Christianity" in all of its facets. Some "gay Christians" have identified more with the welcoming revisions of affirming theology, others with the iconoclastic deconstruction of queer theology, and

---

1. Caryle Murphy, "Lesbian, Gay and Bisexual Americans Differ from General Public in Their Religious Affiliations," Pew Research Center, May 26, 2015, https://www.pewresearch.org/fact-tank/2015/05/26/lesbian-gay-and-bisexual-americans-differ-from-general-public-in-their-religious-affiliations/.

2. "A Survey of LGBT Americans," Pew Research Center, June 13, 2013, https://www.pewsocialtrends.org/2013/06/13/a-survey-of-lgbt-americans/#religion.

still others with the historically orthodox-sounding nuance of gay celibate theology. While these ideas have been held individually for years, there is more and more push for these concepts to be approved and taught corporately by established churches and denominations. In this scenario, inclusion becomes not just an aspiration but a measure of faithfulness.

"Gay Christians" have come to think of inclusion as extending well beyond theological statements. For them, the posture and tone of the church need to exude inclusion and must be expressed practically in the visible make-up of the church membership and leaders. From there, how churches utilize language, combat heteronormativity, and resist homophobia gain increased scrutiny. As we shall see, this re-thinking of the church's visible representation is part of a weakening of the church's commission and calling.

## LGBT Representation and Visibility

*There can be no turning back from the goal of the full partici-pation of lesbian, gay, bisexual, and transgender people in our faith traditions and communities. . . . Loving, just communities embrace everyone; they are strengthened when all people are able to live fully and express their gender and sexuality with holiness and integrity. We celebrate sexual and gender diversity as a blessing that enriches all.* — The Religious Institute on Sexual Morality, Justice, and Healing[3]

---

3. "An Open Letter to Religious Leaders on Sexual and Gender Diversity," The Religious Institute on Sexual Morality, Justice, and Healing, 2007, http://

Just as one of the fundamental goals of the LGBT movement is to normalize queerness in society, one of the fundamental goals of "gay Christianity" is to normalize queerness in the church. There are many facets to this, but one major aspect is having queer people be actively involved in the congregation, ministry staff, and leadership of local churches and Christian ministries. The reasons behind this are summarized in two sociological concepts: representation and visibility.

Through greater LGBT *representation* in church life, queer people are expected to feel more normal and more accepted. This principle was originally developed in relation to popular culture and media depictions, but it applies well beyond that. Psychologist Jennifer O'Brien explains:

> *When people see representations of themselves in the media, this can foster a great sense of affirmation of their identity. Feeling affirmed with one's own sense of self can boost positive feelings of self-worth, which is quite different than feeling as if you are wrong or bad for being who you are.*[4]

If LGBT people can see other LGBT people involved in the life of the church, that increases their own sense of self-worth and willingness to participate in religion and spirituality. They can feel affirmed and accepted by God because they feel affirmed and accepted by people who call themselves Christians.

---

religiousinstitute.org/wp-content/uploads/2009/06/diversityopenletter.pdf.

4. Jennifer O'Brien, "Why Visibility Matters: The Impact of the Rise of LGBTQ+ Representation in Media," *Psychology Today,* November 14, 2017, https://www. psychologytoday.com/us/blog/all-things-lgbtq/201711/why-visibility-matters.

Through greater LGBT *visibility* in church life, straight people are likewise expected to shift how they view gay and transgender people. O'Brien notes this as well: "When people are able to see something represented, they are better able to understand and grasp who those people are, and this creates an important shift in the social consciousness to include people from a range of different backgrounds."[5] If straight people can see happy, normal-looking LGBT people in the church, they will become more sympathetic to LGBT political causes and more likely to push against the "culture war" Christianity of conservative evangelicals.

Visibility also extends to how openly a church shows its support of LGBT causes. Flying a Pride Flag, taking on the moniker "open and affirming," sponsoring floats or booths at Pride Parades, and making public statements endorsing pro-LGBT legislation are all aspects of this. Perhaps the most striking attempt at normalization and visibility is in establishing queer-specific worship services. As National Coming Out Day (in October) has gained more recognition, many affirming churches have sought to do something special during their worship service to recognize congregants who have come out as lesbian, gay, bisexual, or transgender. Some churches have special "Transgender Renaming Services" where the recently transitioned parishioner is honored and commemorated in front of the congregation. During Pride Month (June), many affirming churches have sought to include queer liturgies and responsive readings to repent of the homophobia of the broader church and invoke a more inclusive atmosphere.

---

5. Ibid.

Church assessments and inclusivity workshops have also become popular tools for helping churches become more visibly inclusive. The National LGBTQ Task Force put together "A Welcoming Toolkit," which is a 60-page packet of congregational assessments, worksheets, process outlines, recommended readings, and optimal language for churches to adopt in their public statements regarding LGBT issues. Although it presents initially as gentle guidance for churches who want to hold a workshop on inclusivity, it builds a front-to-back plan for leading a church into full, vocal affirmation—including guidance on finding key church members who can sway opinions to help ensure a successful transition to become more affirming.[6]

These pushes for gay representation are not just a feature of affirming churches, however. "Gay celibate Christians" also embrace many of the same notions, although they may frame them differently. For instance, Living Out, a UK-based ministry that promotes "gay celibate Christianity," released a Church Audit in 2018 intended to help conservative churches discover if they are "biblically inclusive." In addition to leaving their loaded terminology undefined, the audit has church leaders examine themselves to make sure that church meetings always include people who identify as LGBT or are same-sex attracted and that sexual orientation "would never prevent them from exercising their spiritual gifts or serving in leadership in your church."[7]

---

6. "Building an Inclusive Church: A Welcoming Toolkit 2.0," National Gay and Lesbian Task Force Institute for Welcoming Resources, 2009, 2013, 6, http://www.welcomingresources.org/welcomingtoolkit.pdf.

7. "How Biblically Inclusive Is Your Church?" Living Out, 2019, https://www.livingout.org/UserFiles/File/Living_Out_Church_Audit_2019.pdf.

Ed Shaw, a same-sex attracted pastor with Living Out, further explains, "If there's nobody in your church family who [has] been open—perhaps even in private—with you [about their sexual orientation or LGBT identity], you failed the first test."[8] Even though Living Out promotes celibacy rather than homosexual marriage, their language and thinking are still built upon secular ideology, buying into the world's accusation that evangelical churches need to have greater LGBT representation and visibility. It is still an attempt at mainstreaming homosexuality among Bible-believing Christians—one that was heartily endorsed by noted evangelical minister Tim Keller and his wife Kathy at the Living Out Conference in June 2018.[9]

What Christian doesn't want to be part of a loving and just church? But as the Religious Institute quote defines them, loving and just communities are specifically those that "embrace everyone." The word *embrace* has been filled with additional meanings and expectations that run counter to scriptural commands. It implies that a church must celebrate LGBT identity, that it must do nothing to hinder that expression but must do everything in its power to promote it and even bless it. Therefore, the biblical stipulations that church leaders must be holy and above reproach (1 Timothy 3:2) and church members must be Christians who refrain from sexual immorality (1 Thessalonians 4:3–8) suddenly become "harmful" and "bigoted" ideas when they are only

---

8. Ed Shaw, "Introduction to Living Out Church Audit: How Biblically Inclusive Is Your Church?" from Living Out, July 20, 2018, https://vimeo.com/280927726.

9. Ed Shaw, "How Biblically Inclusive Is Your Church? The Living Out Church Audit." Living Out, January 21, 2021, https://www.livingout.org/resources/articles/65/how-biblically-inclusive-is-your-church-the-living-out-church-audit.

the clear teaching of scripture applied to the local church.

Of course, this isn't about a gay person being unwelcome to come and hear the gospel preached on a Sunday morning; all biblical Christians desire for nonbelievers to hear the truth proclaimed. This isn't about keeping people who think they are gay from being able to talk to a pastor or church member about it. This isn't about people being unable to be honest about their struggles with sin. This is about the specific expectations put on those interactions by people who oppose God's design and God's Word. The call for sinners to repent is replaced with the call for Christians to "embrace."

Sexual immorality is not a blessing to the body of Christ—no matter how definitive psychologists believe it is to a person. In fact, if it is embraced and celebrated, it will bring God's judgment (Revelation 2:20–23) and the removal of the Holy Spirit's work from the midst of the church (Revelation 2:5). Some churches embrace this out of a seemingly benign desire to be nice, but at root is a desperate desire for the world's approval. Pride, arrogance, and unbelief lie hidden underneath. Wherever homosexuality is embraced, it will always weaken that church's commitment to scriptural authority and it will further weaken the clarity with which the church's leaders and members understand the grace and power of Almighty God.

## The Language of LGBT Validation

*We believe some people have experienced the use of language and the images they convey as barriers to acknowledging that they are created in God's own image. These people need faithful and inviting language about God which welcomes them as full and complete children of God.* — from an "Inclusive Language Covenant" written by the United Church of Christ[10]

Affirming churches, by definition, want to affirm. They have sought to replace the negative feelings of shame and stigma with more positive feelings of acceptance, affirmation, and validation. Inclusion is now the order of the day. It isn't enough to change our posture; we must also change our language. Some progressives call this the church's *welcome.* The website for the Unitarian Universalist Association states:

> *One of the most public ways that your congregation can proclaim its welcome to all people, regardless of identity, is to include language in your mission statement, bylaws, orders of service, website, newsletter, and so on, that clearly states this welcome.*[11]

Corresponding with this welcome is the push to use *inclusive language* to help people feel comfortable in their

---

10. "Inclusive Language Covenant," United Church of Christ, 1993, https://www.ucc.org/worship/inclusive-language/inclusive-language-covenant.html.

11. "Welcome, Inclusion, Affirmation, and Nondiscrimination Statements," Unitarian Universalist Association, accessed August 9, 2021, https://www.uua.org/lgbtq/welcoming/ways/185991.shtml.

sexuality and gender identity. In other words, do not assume that heterosexuality is normal and that gender is fixed—instead, refer to "people of all sexualities, gender identities, and expressions." Do not assume that a family is a mother and father—refer instead to "parents" or "caregivers." Common Christian greetings like "brothers and sisters" should be replaced by "children of God." Even referring to God in the masculine "He/Him/His" (as the Bible does) is considered problematic, and feminine descriptions of God such as "Mother," "Midwife" or "Mother Hen" are being embraced instead. "The prevalent worship of an exclusively male Supreme Being is the strongest support imaginable for the dominance of men," argues feminist theologian Jann Aldredge-Clanton. "Exclusive worship language and images oppress people by devaluing those excluded."[12]

This is why the push for inclusive language will not end merely with a feminine god but with a queer god. One "queer call to worship" spoke to God this way:

*Strange One. Fabulous One. Fluid and ever becoming One. . . . You are mother, father, and parent. You are sister, brother, and sibling. You are drag queen, and trans man, and gender-fluid—incapable of limiting your vast expressions of beauty. Embodied in us, your creation, we recognize our flesh in all its forms is made holy in You. With thanksgiving, we celebrate your manifestation in all its glorious forms.*[13]

---

12. Jann Aldredge-Clanton, "Why Is Inclusive Language Still Important," Progressive Christianity, December 17, 2013, https://progressivechristianity.org/resources/why-is-inclusive-language-still-important/.

13. "A Queer Call to Worship (1)," enfleshed, accessed August 9, 2021, https://enfleshed.com/liturgy/lgbtq-related/.

This type of liturgical blasphemy is celebrated by many in progressive circles as a step forward toward full LGBT inclusion and validation.

This desire to remove shame from homosexuality has led many to embrace more inclusive worship materials. For instance, in 2012, *The Queen James Bible* was published as a way of "correcting" the texts that spoke about homosexuality based on affirming theology so that LGBT people would have a more comfortable Bible to read during public worship or personal devotion. The Bible features a large rainbow cross on the cover. In 2019, the Hymn Society in the U.S. and Canada released *Songs for the Holy Other: Hymns Affirming the LGBTQIA2S+ Community*. This collection of hymns was intended to make queer hymns like "God of Queer Transgressive Spaces," "Transfigure Me," or "We Are a Rainbow" more accessible to congregations.

There are many ways that language has been softened, adjusted, or shifted in our culture over the years to minimize the shame of the sin of homosexuality. For instance, even the term *homosexual* is now considered offensive. GLAAD lists it as a "term to avoid" on their Media Guide because it is an "outdated clinical term" and "it is aggressively used by anti-LGBTQ extremists to suggest that people attracted to the same sex are somehow diseased or psychologically/emotionally disordered."[14] Instead, the terms *gay and lesbian* or *gay people* are now preferred. Included on their list of defamatory terms (along with more obvious slurs)

---

14. "GLAAD Media Reference Guide." GLAAD, October 2016, 7–9, https://www.glaad.org/sites/default/files/GLAAD-Media-Reference-Guide-Tenth-Edition.pdf.

are biblically motivated words such as *deviant*, *disordered*, *perverted*, *destructive*, and *sodomite*. It is quite obvious that when these are the parameters of language laid down by LGBT activists, conservative churches and leaders will find themselves increasingly in the crosshairs—from outside the church as well as within.

What does it look like when the language surrounding this subject gets softened in conservative circles? Simply consider the way *same-sex attraction* has become the preferre d term for conservative Christians to describe homosexual desire because it speaks more neutrally of homosexuality than other terms that might connote sin or temptation. Though *same-sex attraction* may be descriptive of what people feel like in their experience, it is a phrase that removes the moral framework that Paul embeds in the term *dishonorable passions* (Romans 1:26). Instead, the term *same-sex attraction* is a delicate concession to godless psychology that has assumed "homosexual orientation" is inborn and unchangeable. Instead of "same-sex attraction," why not speak about "homosexual temptation"? As pastor Tim Bayly observes, "It is the difference between saying, 'This is the way I am,' and, 'This is one of the ways I'm tempted.'"[15]

Interestingly, there are those, like gay celibate author Greg Coles, who believe the term *same-sex attraction* is confusing and off-putting to unbelievers—sounding like "impenetrable Christianese." He says that *same-sex attracted* does not clearly communicate that a person is attracted to members of the same sex. He would prefer that the more

---

15. Tim Bayly, Joseph Bayly, and Jürgen Hagen, *The Grace of Shame: 7 Ways the Church Has Failed to Love Homosexuals* (Bloomington, IN: Warhorn Media, 2017), 91.

popular term *gay* be used instead because gay is "a disruptive term in these [evangelical] circles."[16]

"Words matter," the LGBT activists tell us. Yet what they mean is that words matter for making people feel included, for erasing shame, for building acceptance of homosexuality, and for minimizing God. Christians need to be aware that postmodern thought has waged an all-out war on language. It has raised questions about *epistemology* (how we know what we know) and *hermeneutics* (interpreting text) that lead to deeper questions about the nature of *meaning* and the nature of *being*.

The LGBT movement continues to play a prominent role in the devaluing of language so that the very existence of *queerness* stands as a supposedly self-evident protest against traditional understandings and accepted meanings. Words like *gay*, *homosexual*, *attraction*, *discrimination*, and *inclusion* are now filled with *lived experience* rather than empirical meaning, which means that we may no longer be speaking the same language even with commonly assumed dictionary definitions. Adjusting language to appeal to a constantly shifting playbook is foolish. "A fool's mouth is his ruin, and his lips are a snare to his soul" (Proverbs 18:7).

Our language as Christians needs to be grounded in biblical truth; using biblical language is one of the ways we do that. This does not mean that our language must exclusively consist of words and phrases we find in the Bible, but it does mean that our understanding of reality should be

---

16. Greg Coles, "Three Concerns with the Term 'Same-Sex Attracted,'" The Center for Faith, Sexuality & Gender (blog), February 19, 2019, https://www.centerforfaith.com/blog/three-concerns-with-the-term-same-sex-attracted.

shaped and regulated by the language the Bible uses. After all, we know that God's word is true (John 17:17), it is profitable to equip us for good works (2 Timothy 3:16–17), it is everlasting (Isaiah 40:6–8), and it is powerful to accomplish spiritual work in us and through us (Hebrews 4:12).

Paul exhorts Timothy to follow the pattern of "sound words" that he heard from the apostle (1 Timothy 1:13), and Christ warns us that we will be judged for every careless word we speak (Matthew 12:36–37). Pastors spiritually shape their people by the language they use, and the people likewise shape one another (Ephesians 4:29). The world understands this—which is why language and terminology are focal points of activism. In light of this, Christians must be mindful of the dangerous compromises that even well-meaning shifts in language may bring with them.

## Queering the Bible

The Queer God *is a book about this re-discovery of God outside the heterosexual ideology which has been prevalent in the history of Christianity and theology. In order to do that, it is necessary to facilitate the coming out of the closet of God by a process of theological queering.* — Marcella Althaus-Reid, queer theologian[17]

One of the most troubling and blasphemous attempts to recast biblical language is an exercise called *queering* or *queer*

---

17. Marcella Althaus-Reid, *The Queer God* (New York and London: Routledge, 2003), 2.

*reading.* This is a literary technique that was developed in queer theory and is specifically intended to read "queer experience" into texts where it is not typically found in order to offer a challenge to what theorists call *heteronormativity* (the worldview that heterosexuality is normal). As feminist theologian Ellen T. Armour explains:

> *To "queer" is to complicate, to disrupt, to disturb all kinds of orthodoxies, including, at least, these two (often intertwined in current debate): those that take our current sex/gender regime as natural and God-given and those that posit "the Bible" as a flat, transparent window into the divine mind.*[18]

With this explanation clearly outlining the prerogatives of the exercise, it is no wonder that many queer readings of scripture are particularly outlandish and sometimes near pornographic.

For the queer reader, the Bible is not grounded in historical reality but is mostly metaphorical. Its stories and language are viewed through contemporary theoretical lenses and become an expression of queer theology. For example, the account of Jesus healing a demoniac in Luke 8:26–39, when queered, becomes a metaphor for how "Jesus wants us to come out and embrace our God-given identity and truth in order to use our queerness as a gift to preach the gospel and contribute to the liberation of others."[19] A queer reading of Genesis 50:23–25 sees Joseph's desire that his bones be taken

---

18. Ellen T. Armour, "Queer Bibles, Queer Scriptures? An Introductory Response," *Bible Trouble: Queer Reading at the Boundaries of Biblical Scholarship,* eds. Teresa J. Hornsby and Ken Stone (Atlanta, GA: Society of Biblical Literature, 2011), 2.

19. "Queering the Kingdom," The Word Made Queer, accessed August 9, 2021, https://www.wordmadequeer.com/essays/queering-the-kingdon.

to the Promised Land not as an example of Joseph's faith in God (as Hebrews 11:22 understands it), but as a metaphor for the need to preserve the history of LGBT people.[20]

A queer reading of the golden calf in Exodus 32:4–6 is not about rebellious idolatry; instead, it becomes a story about how the sensual exuberance of the people's idol worship was suppressed by the giving of the Mosaic law. As one queer reader reflects, "I was always taught to judge these sinners harshly, but now, as I imagined myself dancing with them, I discovered another angle . . . a subversive message that offers a compelling fusion of sex and spirit, body and soul."[21] In other words, through his enjoyment of sensual pleasure, he now sees sexual immorality and idolatry as aspects of true worship.

Though the queering cited above may not reach beyond a very academic audience, the impact of *queering the Bible* as a practice can be felt at multiple points across our culture. Perhaps the most obvious points of contact are short, evocative statements about the Bible that might be posted on social media that can be easily seen, liked, and shared. For instance, in 2013, a picture of a church sign in Canada went viral. The sign simply said: "Jesus Had Two Dads and He Turned Out Just Fine!"[22] This statement is, effectively, a queer

20. Jill Hammer, "Uncovering Joseph's Bones: Parashat Vayechi (Genesis 47:28–50:26)," *Torah Queeries: Weekly Commentaries on the Hebrew Bible*, eds. Gregg Drinkwater, Joshua Lesser, and David Shneer (New York: New York University Press, 2009), 71.

21. Amichai Lau-Lavie, "Mounting Sinai: Parashat Ki Tisa (Exodus 30:11–34:35)." *Torah Queeries: Weekly Commentaries on the Hebrew Bible*, eds. Gregg Drinkwater, Joshua Lesser, and David Shneer (New York: New York University Press, 2009), 109.

22. Joseph McCormick, "Church Sign Goes Viral: 'Jesus Had Two Dads and He Turned Out Just Fine,'" Pink News, August 30, 2013, https://www.pinknews.co.uk/2013/08/30/church-sign-goes-viral-jesus-had-two-dads-and-he-turned-out-just-fine/.

read on the incarnation—the fact that Christ is divinely the Son of God (Matthew 3:17) and also born physically into Joseph's family (Luke 3:23). It doesn't present an actual theological argument—it merely hints, suggests, and disrupts the way a Christian might think of the natural family, while also creating an openness to the political cause of gay adoption.

But this is all part of the cause. One Bible professor describes why she believes queer reading is an important aspect of biblical criticism:

> *By positioning themselves as interrogators, they [queer readers] consciously stand "outside" to chip away at the "center." The political and social agenda of bringing down heteronormativity (an agenda that I share) is the primary aim of these authors, and it seems to me that the biblical text and other cultural media are tools, or the means by which the political agenda is addressed.*[23]

The influence of queer reading reaches into conservative circles as well. For instance, at the 2018 Revoice Conference (a conference for "gay celibate Christians"), Nate Collins gave what sounds eerily close to a queer reading of Jeremiah 15:15–16 at the end of his message:

> *Is it possible that gay people today are being sent by God, like Jeremiah, to find God's words for the church, to eat them and make them our own, to shed light on contemporary false*

---

23. S. Tamar Kamionkowski, "Queer Theory and Historical-Critical Exegesis: Queering Biblicists—A Response," *Bible Trouble: Queer Reading at the Boundaries of Biblical Scholarship*, eds. Teresa J. Hornsby and Ken Stone (Atlanta, GA: Society of Biblical Literature, 2011), 132.

*teachings and even idolatries, not just the false teaching of the progressive sexual ethic, but other more subtle forms of false teaching? Is it possible that gender and sexual minorities who've lived lives of costly obedience are themselves a prophetic call to the church to abandon idolatrous attitudes toward the nuclear family, toward sexual pleasure? If so, then we are prophets.*[24]

Collins presents his thoughts as a hypothetical, but the hint, suggestion, and disruption of his statements are intended to empower his audience of "gay celibate Christians" to think of themselves as prophets who, by their innate existence as "gender and sexual minorities," are to stand against the "false teachings" of the church. And what are these false teachings? On the one hand they might include the "progressive sexual ethic," but on the other hand, what seems to be most pressing are "more subtle" conservative views: that homosexual orientation is sinful, gay people can change, natural marriage should be promoted, systemic homophobia is an overblown accusation, and Christians should push back against LGBT activism in society.[25] Whereas Jeremiah called the people of Judah to return to God, Nate Collins is calling "gay Christians" to declare that they have been personally slighted by the rest of the church. He does not present scripture as a mere metaphor in the way queer readers typically do, yet his

---

24. Nate Collins, "Revoice 18—General Session 2: Lament | Nate Collins & Ray," from Revoice, August 2, 2018, https://youtu.be/SHe2y2SVjIc.

25. Collins's book *All But Invisible* (Zondervan, 2017) offers more detailed challenges to theological conservatives on each of these points. His writing can sometimes be ambiguous as he tries to find a "third way" between progressive affirmation and biblical conservativism.

application ends up in the same place.

Much debate has occurred in conservative circles about how much the social sciences should inform Christian thinking, with Christians trying to find ways of reconciling certain theoretical assertions with biblical revelation. Many people assume that they can simply take on a secular ideology so long as they add God to the mix or remove the "humanistic trappings" of the worldly thinking.[26] Yet if "the whole world lies under the power of the evil one" (1 John 5:19), why would we think it a harmless thing to take on its way of thinking? "See to it that no one takes you captive through philosophy and empty deceit, according to human tradition, according to the elemental spirits of the universe, and not according to Christ" (Colossians 2:8).

Noted theologian and apologist Norman Geisler—expounding upon that verse—once issued a warning to evangelical scholars to be careful of the damaging ideologies and "alien systems of thought that have invaded Christianity down through the centuries."[27] He cautioned, "Do not see how far the borders of evangelicalism can be stretched to accommodate the latest scholarly fad. Do not flirt with the latest critical methodology."[28] As Geisler and many other sound theologians have recognized over the years, when people become enamored with worldly theories and philosophies, those theories inevitably become lenses through which

---

26. Nate Collins, *All But Invisible: Exploring Identity Questions at the Intersection of Faith, Gender, and Sexuality* (Grand Rapids, MI: Zondervan, 2017), 259.

27. Norman L. Geisler, "Beware of Philosophy: A Warning to Biblical Scholars," *Journal of the Evangelical Theological Society (JETS)* 42, no. 1 (March 1999): 3, https://www.etsjets.org/files/JETS-PDFs/42/42-1/42-1-pp003-019_JETS.pdf.

28. Ibid., 15.

the scriptures are read. They can—and often will—lead to an altering of the very message of scripture.

## The Weapon of Homophobia

*Homophobia can take many different forms, including negative attitudes and beliefs about, aversion to, or prejudice against bisexual, lesbian, and gay people. It's often based in irrational fear and misunderstanding. Some people's homophobia may be rooted in conservative religious beliefs. People may hold homophobic beliefs if they were taught them by parents and families.* — Planned Parenthood's website[29]

Where churches are slow or unwilling to adopt any change in theology or representation, it is inevitable that activists will blame *homophobia* as the root cause for their resistance. After all, why do LGBT people and the church seem perpetually at odds? There has to be underlying discrimination and prejudice, right? Obviously, no one wants to be perceived as a bigot—especially people whose entire ethos is built around loving God and loving others. So Christians naturally object to the claim, but it doesn't seem to matter what Christians say or do—the charge of homophobia always emerges. Is there any truth to the claim? Are Christians really unkind or unjust—as a principle—to LGBT people? Before we can

29. "What Is Homophobia?" Planned Parenthood, accessed August 9, 2021, https://www.plannedparenthood.org/learn/sexual-orientation/sexual-orientation/what-homophobia.

answer that question, we must first know what *homophobia* means and how the term has changed over the years.

The concept of homophobia was originally developed in the mid-1960s by secular psychologist George Weinberg, and he is credited with coining the term in the early 1970s. It entered the mainstream with the publication of his book *Society and the Healthy Homosexual* (1972). Weinberg believed there was an actual psychological phobia that he had seen demonstrated in some of his patients, so he defined *homophobia* as "the dread of being in close quarters with homosexuals—and in the case of homosexuals themselves, self-loathing."[30] He believed this fear often expressed itself in prejudice—whether in aversion, loathing, jokes, belittling statements, or anger and aggression toward homosexuals. Weinberg saw many psychological causes underneath homophobia, but he also believed it was shaped by the Judeo-Christian worldview that undergirded much of Western culture.[31]

The influential book *Is the Homosexual My Neighbor?* (originally written in 1978; revised and updated in 1994) by Letha Dawson Scanzoni and Virginia Ramey Mollenkott took Weinberg's definition of *homophobia* and expanded it to include ignorance, insensitivity, stereotypical expectations, and lack of personal interaction with homosexuals. Their goal was to present social data that combated gay stereotypes while also casting doubt on traditional interpretations of scripture by making it seem as if conservatives had been shutting themselves out from the truth due to fear. They wrote:

---

30. George Weinberg, *Society and the Healthy Homosexual* (Garden City, NY: Anchor Press/Doubleday, 1972), 4.

31. Ibid., 8–10.

*Our hope in writing this book is that many of our readers will be willing to examine the evidence and correct any misconceptions they may have held about gay, lesbian, and bisexual people, learning to love all their neighbors as themselves.*[32]

With clever appeals to other scriptural truths such as loving your neighbor, Scanzoni and Mollenkott provided much of the framework for "gay Christian" arguments going forward.

The emergence of the term *homophobia* seemed to crystalize a feeling of rejection in homosexuals' experience of society. Gay and lesbian activists took the word and ran with it—using the term to reframe the "social problem" of homosexuality altogether. Whereas "the problem of homosexuality" had once been framed in terms of illicit sexual behavior, mental illness, destructive lifestyle choices, and moral sinfulness, *homophobia* implied that the real problem was the discrimination and stigma of homosexuals by "heterosexual society." This is what some theorists have labelled *systemic homophobia*, *heterosexism*, or *heteronormativity*. In popular use, *homophobia* eventually came to be used alongside *sexism* and *racism* as an umbrella term for any discrimination against LGBT people. This is because homosexuality is seen as so intrinsic to who a person is that to say or do anything against homosexuality is the equivalent of civil rights discrimination against an entire class of people.

The term continues to have a potent gut response attached

---

32. Letha Dawson Scanzoni and Virginia Ramey Mollenkott, *Is the Homosexual My Neighbor? A Positive Christian Response,* rev. ed. (New York, NY: HarperCollins, 1994), 158.

to it—similar to the charge of racism. Yet even activist scholars like Gregory Herek have had to admit that *homophobia* has limitations when it comes to conservative Christians:

> *Most of them do not have a debilitating fear of homosexuality (although they often try to evoke fear to promote their political agenda). Rather, they are hostile to gay people and gay communities, and condemn homosexual behavior as sinful, unnatural, and sick. Whereas this stance is not necessarily a phobia, it clearly qualifies as a prejudice. It is a set of negative attitudes toward people based on their membership in the group homosexual or gay or lesbian.*[33]

Herek proposed that scholars and activists start using terms such as *sexual stigma*, *heterosexism*, and *sexual prejudice* to implicate Christians because their religious values and support for "antigay organizations" were the real threat. "Labeling them homophobic obscures the true sources of their hostility."[34]

The refusal to capitulate on LGBT political causes, in particular, garners vehement attacks, as this becomes the central evidence in the case against the church. According to People for the American Way, the "homophobia" of politically active conservative Christians is most clearly evidenced in the policies they are willing to support and those they are not:

33. Gregory M. Herek, "Beyond 'Homophobia': Thinking about Sexual Prejudice and Stigma in the Twenty-First Century," National Sexuality Resource Center, *Journal of NRSC* 1, no. 2 (April 2004), 17, https://psychology.ucdavis.edu/rainbow/html/Herek_2004_SRSP.pdf.

34. Ibid., 13.

*Anti-gay politics have long been at the core of Religious Right fundraising and organizing efforts. As the Religious Right becomes an increasingly powerful element of the GOP base, anti-gay rhetoric and policies have become more prominent in party platforms, legislative fights, and public policy at local, state, and national levels.*[35]

It is a matter of how conservative politics are framed. In this scenario, a person either supports "gay rights" or is "anti-gay." Pushing against pro-gay legislation is seen as an expression of discrimination and is thereby homophobic. From there anyone can read fear, hatred, ignorance, or any other negative connotation they want into the term *homophobic;* and the charge, in the court of public opinion, is likely to stick. An article in *Psychology Today* illustrates this sentiment in no uncertain terms:

*In seeking to follow these ancient scriptures, strong Christians actively fight to deny homosexuals the right to live freely: to marry who they want, to raise children, to teach in public schools, to have legal protection from discrimination, etc. Not very kind, not very loving—to say the least. But that's what happens when one's "morality" is based on obedience to a magical being.*[36]

---

35. "Anti-Gay Politics and the Religious Right," People for the American Way, August 2002, https://www.pfaw.org/report/anti-gay-politics-and-the-religious-right/.

36. Phil Zuckerman, "Religion, Secularism, and Homophobia: One Reason Why Younger Americans Are Fleeing the Faith," *Psychology Today,* July 21, 2017, https://www.psychologytoday.com/us/blog/the-secular-life/201707/religion-secularism-and-homophobia.

So we are left with this question: Are conservative Christians homophobic? Accusing the church of homophobia has been a complicated and mixed charge. On the one hand, there is no question that the term *homophobia* has been weaponized by LGBT activists to either force a change in Christian doctrine or silence the church's faithful public witness on sexuality altogether. The term has become increasingly vague over the years as the actual fear of homosexuals has subsided culturally. On the other hand, it can rightly be said that some Christians have been harsh, unloving, or antagonistic in their attitude toward homosexuals as people. This response is sinful and requires repentance. But it all depends on what someone is actually talking about when they speak of *homophobia*.

Many Christians who have ministered to homosexuals over the years have found the need to address what could be called an *attitude of homophobia* among professing Christians. In 1984, former homosexual Sy Rogers warned:

> *If you are having a difficult time dealing with any person because of his homosexuality, then you need to take a look at your attitude—and get it right. Being squeamish about homosexuality is one thing. But having a reaction of revulsion, hostility or violence toward the gay person is sin.*[37]

In 1978, conservative Presbyterian pastor Jerry Kirk encouraged Christians to remember their calling as ambassadors of Christ to a lost and dying world:

---

37. Sy Rogers, "When Someone You Love Is Gay," First Stone Ministries, January 21, 1999 (original copyright 1984, Love in Action), https://www.firststone.org/articles/post/when-someone-you-love-is-gay.

*The homosexual has sinned. But Christian, your sin of lovelessness may be keeping him from finding hope and Christ. He may not as yet have found a Christian who will love him as he is and guide him to wholeness in Christ.*[38]

As former homosexual Stephen Black reminds us:

*The Gospel according to Jesus Christ is the same message for a gay-identified person, an idolater, an adulterer, a fornicator, a pornographer, a liar, a thief, a gossip, a slanderer or a murderer. The message of good news—redemption into a love relationship with God—is the same for all sinners.*[39]

These statements testify to the need for personal self-examination (Psalm 139:23–24) as well as grief-filled compassion in our hearts toward others (Romans 9:1–3). Yet not every case of so-called discrimination by Christians is done out of fear, anger, or revulsion. Holding to the clear biblical teaching that homosexuality is sinful is not unloving or unkind or something that requires repentance. In fact, it is the affirming position that lies about God's Word and God's character, and those who spread those lies will not be held guiltless (Jeremiah 23:29–32).

Because homosexuality is wicked and defiling, Christians are right to be disgusted at its normalization and celebration (Isaiah 5:20). We are also right to be disgusted by

---

38. Jerry R. Kirk, *The Homosexual Crisis in the Mainline Church* (Nashville, TN: Thomas Nelson Publishers, 1978), 125.

39. Stephen Black, "The Gospel According to Jesus Christ; and the 'Gay Christian?'" August 15, 2011, https://www.stephenblack.org/blog/post/the-gospel-according-to-jesus-christ--and-the--gay-christian-

the shameful act itself; after all, even in the work of exposing sin we should be mindful of the shame attached to wicked deeds. As Ephesians 5:11–12 says, "Take no part in the unfruitful works of darkness, but instead expose them. For it is shameful even to speak of the things that they do in secret." Christians have a calling to contend for the faith (Jude 1:3) while having mercy on those who doubt, trying to pull them from the fire if we can (Jude 1:22–23).

Many Christians have learned to cower at the very accusation of homophobia. They quickly retreat, adding ambiguity to their already confusing explanations of what they believe or how they apply it. Or they just keep silent about the whole issue, not wanting to offend anyone because they don't share a gay person's experience. For these cowards, simple, straightforward questions suddenly become deeply complicated matters. We should remember that Christ Himself warned, "Do not fear those who kill the body but cannot kill the soul. Rather fear him who can destroy both soul and body in hell" (Matthew 10:28).

Christians need to be aware that the cultural crusade against homophobia is not merely a push against people's unkind personal attitudes. It is, in fact, an attempt to completely reshape society—to remove social norms and expectations, to shift moral thinking, to alter ethical values, and to reconstruct the institutions of the family, the church, the government, and the courts. If "homophobia arises from the nature and construction of the political, legal, economic, sexual, racial, and family systems within which we live"—as renowned LGBT activist Urvashi Vaid claims[40]—then, it is argued, the solution is not simply to become more personally sensitive to LGBT people but to aid in the total dismantling and reconfiguring of society as we know it.

If we look carefully, we see that the charge of homophobia is ultimately an attempt to replace the shame of homosexuality with the approval stamp of victimhood. It is an attempt to embolden sexual strugglers to embrace their desires and live however they want. "Give in. Live out. Be who you are." It is speaking "peace, peace" when there is no peace (Jeremiah 6:14), forgetting that those who do not know how to blush will eventually be overthrown by God (Jeremiah 6:15). It is also an attempt to weigh the church down with the burden of fear—fearing that they are wrong, that they have offended, that they are responsible for causing people's suffering and pain.

Christians must not be intimidated by the fact that where repentance is truly preached, many people will turn away sad (Matthew 19:22) or become angry (Luke 4:28–29), for they love their sin and would rather be affirmed in their choices than submit themselves to Christ (James 4:4). "And this is the judgment: the light has come into the world, and people loved the darkness rather than the light because their works were evil" (John 3:19). Faithful Christians will continue to speak the truth in love, showing kindness while also holding firm to the truth of scripture. It is what faithful believers have done and will continue to do until Christ returns.

---

40. Urvashi Vaid, *Virtual Equality: The Mainstreaming of Gay and Lesbian Liberation* (New York, NY: Anchor Books, Doubleday, 1995), 183.

# What's the Problem?

*Worship the Lord in the splendor of holiness; tremble before him, all the earth!* — Psalm 96:9

In the 2009 guide for psychologists entitled *Appropriate Therapeutic Responses to Sexual Orientation,* the American Psychological Association described ideal affirmative care this way: "The empathic therapeutic environment aspires to be a place of compassionate caring and respect that facilitates development by exploring issues without criticism or condemnation and by reducing distress caused by isolation, stigma, and shame."[41] Although this is a secular medical institution describing how psychologists should approach clients, it also encapsulates how many people have come to view the role of the Christian church in relation to LGBT people. Pastors are considered merely "spiritual psychologists" who empathize and explore issues with gay parishioners without criticism or condemnation, while the church body helps them overcome stigma, shame, and isolation through the "inclusive" practices of the church.

Every attempt by affirming churches to create a "safe and inclusive space" for LGBT people assumes that the church primarily exists for human community and well-being. The activities and emphasis of the church are guided by how included and affirmed people feel. But the church does not

41. Judith M. Glassgold et al., *Report of the American Psychological Association Task Force on Appropriate Therapeutic Responses to Sexual Orientation* (Washington, DC: American Psychological Association, 2009), 55, https://www.apa.org/pi/lgbt/resources/therapeutic-response.pdf.

exist primarily for us—it exists for God. He is the One we worship, the One we honor, the One we obey. What if our attempts to adjust His worship to make people feel more comfortable at church are an offense to the One who established the church?

When we worship God, we are ascribing worth to Him. He has commanded that we worship Him exclusively (Exodus 20:3), without the aid of images and idols (Exodus 20:4–6), and without using His name emptily or flippantly (Exodus 20:7). In the New Testament, Christ told us that we must worship God in spirit and truth (John 4:24). We are also told that a life of godly obedience is part of our daily spiritual worship (Romans 12:1). In short, if we do well, our worship is accepted by God; if we do not do well, we are in danger of being consumed by the sin that is crouching at the door (Genesis 4:7).

Furthermore, we are told to beware of false teachers (1 John 4:1), that these teachers will secretly introduce heresies that embrace sensuality (2 Peter 2:1–2), that they will be evident by their ungodly fruit (Matthew 7:16–20), and that they will be sought out when people no longer want to hear sound doctrine taught (2 Timothy 4:3–4). We are even told that those who are sexually immoral who persist in calling themselves our brothers and sisters in Christ should be removed from fellowship (1 Corinthians 5:9–11).

Needless to say, we are not without clear biblical witness in these matters. The problem is that people refuse to heed God's Word. People have imagined themselves wiser, more honest, and more loving than God Himself—the One who is Love and Wisdom and Truth and therefore the One most fit to define those terms for us. God is also holy. When the Religious Institute on Sexual Morality, Justice, and Healing says that homosexuals should be able to express their sexuality "with holiness and integrity," they are speaking sentimental nonsense.[42] There is no personal holiness outside of biblical obedience. There is no way to make a defiling act an expression of holiness and integrity.

Many queer theologians have tried to relate the contemporary idea of *queerness* to the biblical concept of *holiness*—saying that a gay person is *queer* in the same way that God is *holy*. But when the Bible uses the word *holy* to describe God's *otherness*, it is not expressing the idea of *queerness* but the idea of distinct moral purity and righteous intention. For example, 1 John 1:5 says, "God is light, and in him is no darkness at all." In Isaiah 6 when the prophet is allowed to see a vision of God, where the seraphim proclaim that God is "Holy, holy, holy," Isaiah immediately realizes he is unclean before so great and righteous a One as the Lord (Isaiah 6:5).

Holiness, in other words, is about saying there is none like God. It is purity and power, righteousness and truth. Unstained. Undefiled. God's holiness should highlight our unholiness—our unrighteousness, our sinfulness, our inability, our smallness, our limitation. This queering of God seeks to make His holiness a point of camaraderie with sinful humanity. When the Bible speaks about God's holiness, it is what shows us our need; it is not a point we have in common with God because we sometimes feel like outsiders.

---

42. "An Open Letter to Religious Leaders on Sexual and Gender Diversity," The Religious Institute on Sexual Morality, Justice, and Healing, 2007, http://religiousinstitute.org/wp-content/uploads/2009/06/diversityopenletter.pdf.

The progressive church has forgotten the reason the Christian church exists. In fact, progressives seem to hate the Great Commission and the call to repentance. Nevertheless, the call to repentance is crucial. Early in His ministry, Jesus proclaimed, "The time is fulfilled, and the kingdom of God is at hand; repent and believe in the gospel" (Mark 1:15).

The church is not here for human validation and inclusion. The church is here to carry out the work Christ authorized it to do: "Go therefore and make disciples of all nations, baptizing them in the name of the Father and of the Son and of the Holy Spirit, *teaching them to observe all that I have commanded you*" (Matthew 28:19–20; emphasis mine).

Sadly, the progressive church walks as "enemies of the cross of Christ" (Philippians 3:18), refusing to imitate the example of the apostles, marking out their end according to God's decree: "Their end is destruction, their god is their belly, and they glory in their shame, with minds set on earthly things" (Philippians 3:19). But even the most conservative church can fall prey to the same thinking if its people accommodate worldliness in their own hearts and minds.

> *Do not love the world or the things in the world. If anyone loves the world, the love of the Father is not in him. For all that is in the world—the desires of the flesh and the desires of the eyes and pride of life—is not from the Father but is from the world. And the world is passing away along with its desires, but whoever does the will of God abides forever.* (1 John 2:15–17)

Underneath the lie of "gay pride" lies the heart of man's pride. These are not small matters of accommodation; they speak to the true nature of our hearts before God.

# CHAPTER 4

# RETHINKING IDENTITY

When the Bible speaks about homosexuality, it seems most directly to be addressing homosexual intercourse. "You shall not lie with a male as with a woman" (Leviticus 18:22). Clearly gay sex is forbidden. But what about the mental state of being same-sex attracted? Does the Bible say anything about homosexual orientation?

Explanations have arisen in recent years—buoyed by scientific-sounding language—arguing that homosexuality is not fundamentally about the action of homosexual intercourse but about a unique set of inborn desires and attractions that gay people have for members of the same sex. If people are born gay, then that means that homosexuality is, in some sense, completely natural. Likewise, if same-sex attraction is hard-wired into a person's mind (which usually implies a genetic cause), then that attraction is unlikely to ever change. If those things are true, then gay people are a persecuted class of people whose rights are being trampled by the majority who have "normalized" heterosexuality to the exclusion of variant sexual realities. Therefore, it is argued, the Bible is not really applicable in its understanding of homosexuality.

This idea of *sexual orientation* is a fundamental piece of

what makes "gay Christianity" compelling to people in the twenty-first century. It is bolstered by secular psychology and has been enshrined in the sciences as normal. But the push to normalize the language of *sexual orientation* also has political ends in mind. Before we see how this idea impacts the church, we should see where the idea of innate homosexuality first emerged and why it has proven to be such a vital concept in the gay rights movement.

## A Brief History of Sexual Orientation

*To love even the most beautiful woman is absolutely impossible for me, and indeed solely because no woman instills even a trace of love feelings in me; no one, however, can instill love toward certain persons or sexes through his own strength of will. This has also always been so with me.* — Karl Heinrich Ulrichs, nineteenth-century German lawyer now recognized as a pioneer of the modern gay rights movement[1]

Once upon a time, homosexuals were known as *sodomites* (men who engaged in sodomy). The word for homosexual intercourse defined the word for people who engaged in that activity. Across the Western world, sodomy was illegal, and to be known as a sodomite was understood as living in a way that was both wrong and unnatural. The act of homosexual intercourse was sometimes called a "crime against nature."

---

1. Hubert Kennedy, *The Life and Works of Karl Heinrich Ulrichs, Pioneer of the Modern Gay Movement* (Boston: Alyson, 1988), 8. (Citation from an 1862 letter by Karl Heinrich Ulrichs to his sister Ulrike, as documented by Kennedy.)

126

But in 1869, an Austrian-born social reformer named Karl-Maria Kertbeny first coined the word *homosexuality* (in German, *homosexualität*) as a way of opposing antisodomy laws in Prussia by claiming that the desire for sodomy was natural and thereby outside the bounds of the law to prosecute if done in private.

Though similar, the words *homosexuality* and *sodomy* are not synonyms—in fact, the two terms implied differences in how society was coming to think about homosexuality as a phenomenon. One Christian denominational paper succinctly explained this history:

*The shift in terminology was not simply a change of words; it was part of a broader shift in how same-sex issues were coming to be understood. Rather than viewing a person who engages in same-sex activity as acting against the way he or she is "sexually wired" (and thus labeled a sodomite) it was now argued that some people are actually physiologically "wired," sexually, for same-sex desires (and thus are, by nature, homosexual).*[2]

At the same time that Kertbeny was coining the terms *homosexual* and *heterosexual*, a German lawyer named Karl Heinrich Ulrichs was developing a scientific theory of what would much later be called *sexual orientation* to describe his own sexual attraction. He believed he had a female soul inside his male body that made him attracted to men. Ironically,

---

2. "Contemporary Perspectives on Sexual Orientation: A Theological and Pastoral Analysis," *Minutes of the 2011 Synod of the Reformed Presbyterian Church of North America* (Pittsburgh: 2011), 87, http://rparchives.org/data/Minutes%20of%20Synod/2011%20 Minutes.pdf.

he expressed frustration that society was guided more by "poorly understood Bible passages and laws based on such Bible passages" rather than on a science that, he believed, had sought to investigate sexuality more objectively.[3] Though Ulrichs never adopted the term *homosexual* (he preferred his own terminology), his view of homosexuality being inborn was influential.

Shortly afterward, psychiatrist Karl Westphal argued that men and women who were guilty of seeking homosexual intercourse should come under psychiatric care rather than legal prosecution, as they were sufferers of something Westphal called "contrary sexual feeling." Thinking of homosexuality as a mental illness was seen as a progressive idea at the time because it implied that people who committed sodomy were not directly responsible for their actions. Richard von Krafft-Ebing published a book on sexual pathologies in 1886, after which Kertbeny's term was adopted throughout Europe and America. By the early twentieth century, the term *sodomy* had passed out of fashion and was being replaced by *homosexuality* in most medical and legal writing.

In the twentieth century, famous psychoanalyst Sigmund Freud had many theories that contributed to the West's changing attitudes about sex. While Freud's view of homosexuality was not always clear and seemed to change over his career, he was certainly sympathetic to it as a sexual phenomenon. Freud generally held that people were born innately bisexual and developed into either homosexual or

---

3. Hubert Kennedy, *The Life and Works of Karl Heinrich Ulrichs, Pioneer of the Modern Gay Movement* (Boston: Alyson, 1988), 44. (Citation from an 1861 manuscript by Karl Heinrich Ulrichs as documented by Kennedy.)

heterosexual based on formative experiences in sex development. Many writers note that Freud saw homosexuality as "an inhibition of normal development."[4] However, what is debated is to what extent Freud believed homosexuality to be a psychopathology—that is, a mental illness. Toward the end of his life, Freud famously responded to a mother asking about her homosexual son:

> *Homosexuality is assuredly no advantage, but it is nothing to be ashamed of, no vice, no degradation, it cannot be classified as an illness; we consider it to be a variation of the sexual function produced by a certain arrest of sexual development.*[5]

Although some later writers would argue that Freud's views led to tension between homosexuals and the psychological profession, this 1935 letter was widely circulated in the early days of the gay rights movement as evidence that even Sigmund Freud himself said there was nothing wrong with being a homosexual.

Regardless of Freud's exact views on the nature or causes of homosexuality, his emphasis on the subconscious mind was revolutionary. Historian and gay activist John D'Emilio explains, "Despite Freud's postulation of a continuum between constitutional and environmental influences on sexual development, psychoanalysis decisively shifted medical investigation of sexuality to the psyche and away from the body, where

---

4. Kenneth Lewes, *The Psychoanalytic Theory of Male Homosexuality* (New York: Simon & Schuster, 1988), 30.

5. "Freud's 'Letter to a Mother' of 1935," PsychPage, February 2001, http://www.psychpage.com/gay/library/freudsletter.html.

nineteenth-century science had focused its attention."[6]

The man whose work most profoundly shaped the prevailing thinking on sexuality—and paved the way for the forthcoming sexual revolution—was American biologist Alfred Kinsey. In 1948 he published his wildly influential book *Sexual Behavior of the Human Male,* in which he collected and interpreted the sexual histories of 5,300 American men. The research had begun as early as 1935 at Indiana University in Bloomington after Kinsey became convinced that restrictive social mores around sex were harmful to individuals and society.

The research was enthusiastically received, and the book became a bestseller. "The Kinsey survey explodes traditional concepts of what is normal and abnormal, natural and unnatural in sexual behavior," said the *Harper's Magazine* spotlight about the findings.[7] Although Kinsey's research purported to be representative of the "average American male," in reality it was skewed by his heavy reliance on those considered "sexual deviants"—homosexuals, male street prostitutes, prisoners convicted of sex crimes, men who had sex with animals, and pedophiles. For Kinsey, no sex acts were morally wrong or abnormal because they were all "an expression of capacities that are basic in the human animal."[8]

---

6. John D'Emilio, *Sexual Politics, Sexual Communities: The Making of a Homosexual Minority in the United States, 1940–1970* (Chicago, IL: The University of Chicago Press, 1983), 16.

7. Albert Deutsch, "The Sex Habits of American Men: Some of the Findings of the Kinsey Report," *Harper's Magazine,* December 1947, 494, https://kinseyinstitute.org/pdf/Harpers1947.pdf.

8. Alfred Kinsey, Wardell Pomeroy, and Clyde Martin, *Sexual Behavior in the Human Male* (Philadelphia and London: W.B. Saunders, 1948), 666.

This was especially evident in Kinsey's fascination with homosexuality. He never argued for the existence of an innate and immutable sexual orientation. Perhaps Kinsey did imply something to that effect, but psychology was not as important to him as the documentary history of a person's sexual behavior. When dealing with the question of whether homosexual patterns of behavior were inherited, he said, "The recognition of homosexuality in any individual should not be considered sufficient unless a complete sexual history is available."[9] In other words, he thought the real proof of homosexuality wasn't in thoughts and feelings but in action.

For Kinsey, homosexuality was a basic part of humanity in the sense that human beings would always seek out ways to behave sexually—whether those things were approved by society or not. Furthermore, whatever "hereditary mechanisms" might be behind this behavior, Kinsey firmly believed that sexual behavior could always change—from exclusively heterosexual to exclusively homosexual and vice versa—or any other variation in between.[10]

The research Kinsey released did a great deal to socially legitimize homosexual behavior. It made it seem far more common than anyone had previously considered it. For example, he said that 37% of the men he studied claimed to have had at least one "overt homosexual experience," while 10% of males are "more or less exclusively homosexual for at least 3 years."[11] This 10% number became frequently cited by

---

9. Ibid., 662.
10. Ibid., 663.
11. Ibid., 650–651.

activists seeking to prove that homosexuals were a significant portion of the general population.[12]

Perhaps the most striking thing about Kinsey's research was that whether the topic was adultery, homosexuality, bestiality, or pedophilia, the reports were written in a way that avoided moral judgments. For instance, at the conclusion of *Sexual Behavior in the Human Male*, Kinsey says the following:

*The social values of human activities must be measured by many scales other than those which are available to the scientist. Individual responsibilities toward others in the social organization, and the long-range outcome of behavior which represents the individual's response to the stimuli of the immediate moment, are things that persons other than scientists must evaluate. As scientists, we have explored, and we have performed our function when we have published the record of what we have found the human male doing sexually, as far as we have been able to ascertain that fact.*[13]

Yet for all his scientific posturing, Kinsey was not merely reporting data. His studies came with suggestions for how the data about sexual behavior might be applied to

---

12. Activists in the 1970s to1990s often claimed that 10% or more of the general population were gay. However, numerous surveys have found the total population figures to be much lower. In a 2018 survey of a 340,000-person sample, Gallup found that 4.5% of the U.S. population identified as lesbian, gay, bisexual, or transgender. They noted that there was a year-over-year increase in LGBT identification. For instance, in 2012 only 3.5% of the population identified as such. Frank Newport, "In U.S., Estimate of LGBT Population Rises to 4.5%," Gallup, May 22, 2018, https://news.gallup.com/poll/234863/estimate-lgbt-population-rises.aspx.

13. Alfred Kinsey, Wardell Pomeroy, and Clyde Martin, *Sexual Behavior in the Human Male* (Philadelphia and London: W.B. Saunders, 1948), 678.

education, medicine, law, religion, the military, and society at large. He suggested that morals would change if people knew how commonly certain sex acts were practiced because "immorality seems particularly gross to an individual who is unaware of the frequency with which exceptions to the supposed rule actually occur."[14] Indeed, many people used his reports as evidence in court cases to overturn sex laws and change policy in every field.

Even Kinsey's biographer, James H. Jones, had to acknowledge the underlying motivations behind Kinsey's research:

*Kinsey loathed Victorian morality as only a person who had been badly injured by sexual repression could despise it. He was determined to use science to strip human sexuality of its guilt and repression. He wanted to undermine traditional morality, to soften the rules of restraint, and to help people develop positive attitudes toward their sexual needs and desires. Kinsey was a crypto-reformer who spent his every waking hour attempting to change the sexual mores and sex offender laws of the United States. . . . The fact that his methodology and data were flawed in no way diminishes his stature as a pioneer—the researcher who made the public believe not only that science should and could study human sexual behavior but that social policy and the law should be reevaluated in light of scientific data.[15]*

---

14. Ibid., 667.

15. James H. Jones, *Alfred C. Kinsey: A Public/Private Life* (New York: W.W. Norton & Company, 1997), xii—xiii.

Psychoanalysis and psychiatric therapy had grown in popularity in the United States during the twentieth century and had become especially pronounced in the 1950s. The American Psychiatric Association (APA) published its first handbook of mental disorders in 1952. This handbook, called the *Diagnostic and Statistical Manual of Mental Disorders* (DSM), classified homosexuality as a "sociopathic personality disturbance."[16] In other words, the psychiatric establishment considered homosexuality a mental illness. This view was not accepted by everyone, however.

In 1957 and 1958, psychologist Evelyn Hooker—empowered by Kinsey's claim that there was nothing pathological about homosexual behavior—sought to show that there was a false correlation between homosexuality and mental illness. She interviewed 30 heterosexual men and 30 homosexual men who had never sought psychological treatment or been incarcerated, and then gave these unmarked psychological profiles to three psychologists who would try to distinguish between the homosexuals and heterosexuals based on the charts. Her test seemed to prove that homosexuals were not psychologically disturbed.

Hooker's test was widely influential—eventually garneringher the label "The Grande Dame of Gay Liberation" from the *Los Angeles Times*.[17] Yet according to psychiatrists

---

16. Jack Drescher, "Out of DSM: Depathologizing Homosexuality," *Behavior Science*, December 2015, 565–575, https://www.ncbi.nlm.nih.gov/pmc/articles/PMC4695779/.

17. Bruce Shenitz, "The Grande Dame of Gay Liberation: Evelyn Hooker's Friendship with a UCLA Student Spurred Her to Studies That Changed the Way Psychiatrists View Homosexuality," *Los Angeles Times*, June 10, 1990, https://www.latimes.com/archives/la-xpm-1990-06-10-tm-539-story.html.

like Jeffrey B. Satinover, her research methods were inherently flawed:

> *Hooker failed to follow even the most basic tenets of the scientific method. She deliberately had her associates recruit participants to obtain a pool of subjects who understood what the "experiment" was about and how it was to be used to achieve a political goal in transforming society. As she wrote many years later, "I knew the men for whom the ratings were made, and I was certain as a clinician that they were relatively free of psychopathology." In other words, she lacked a random sample and tinkered with the composition of both groups to conform to whatever she defined.*[18]

It was also during the 1950s that *homophile organizations* began to emerge in Los Angeles, San Francisco, and New York City. These were groups where homosexuals could openly socialize with one another, develop a sense of group identity, publish magazines, and begin to organize politically. The term *homophile* was chosen so that love and romance would be emphasized while homosexual intercourse would be de-emphasized. The hope was that this would help homosexuals become more socially accepted and be able to assimilate more easily into mainstream society. In fact, Evelyn Hooker worked closely with a homophile organization to find the right subjects for her study.

---

18. Jeffrey B. Satinover, "The 'Trojan Couch': How the Mental Health Associations Misrepresent Science," *National Association for Research and Therapy of Homosexuality*, 2007, 8. Web archive snapshot from January 17, 2012, https://web.archive.org/web/20120117025036/https://www.narth.com/docs/TheTrojanCouchSatinover.pdf.

What began to emerge from the homophile groups—especially the Mattachine Society, founded by Communist organizer Harry Hay in 1950—was the idea of homosexuals as an "oppressed minority" within society. In its Statement of Purpose from 1951, the Mattachine Society heavily pushed against the accepted notion of homosexuals as moral degenerates or sexual deviants. It said:

> The [Mattachine] Society believes homosexuals can lead well-adjusted, wholesome, and socially productive lives once ignorance, and prejudice, against them is successfully combatted, and once homosexuals themselves feel they have a dignified and useful role to play in society. The Society, to these ends, is in the process of developing a homosexual ethic . . . disciplined, moral, and socially responsible.[19]

Although Hay's group had a radical pedigree, progress was slow and political victories were few. Still, by fostering self-identification as part of an oppressed minority, the homophile groups had an impact within the homosexual subculture. By the 1960s, younger gay activists—seeing the steady progress being made for African-Americans in the Civil Rights movement—were growing restless about their own situation. These frustrations bubbled over in the earth-shaking event that would be known as the Stonewall Riots.

On June 27, 1969, police raided a gay bar in Greenwich Village called the Stonewall Inn. While this was not an infrequent practice by New York City police, this particular raid

---

19. Van Grosse, *The Movements of the New Left, 1950-1975* (Boston, MA: Bedford/St. Martin's, 2005), 40.

was not taken peacefully. Gay historian Fred Fejes explains the riots and their immediate influence:

*Instead of meekly submitting to police arrests, bar patrons [at Stonewall Inn] fought back, and the episode quickly escalated into two nights of riotous protests involving four hundred police and over two thousand gay protesters. Inspired by the riots, gay radical activists in Greenwich Village began organizing. One month later over three hundred people rallied in Washington Square Park, where "the homosexual revolution" was proclaimed.*[20]

The Stonewall Riots defined the focus and intensity of gay activism going forward in America. Yet there was a major limitation to the social acceptance of homosexuality— the fact that psychiatry and psychology still treated homosexuality as a mental illness. This was the next target of gay activists. One historical summary says:

*Before the Stonewall riots, homophile groups had accepted the medical view of homosexuality as a mental disorder. Their view had been that accepting homosexuality as [a] disease meant treating it as a disability, rather than a moral or religious sin, and would lead to more objective and humane attitudes. A new generation of gay rights activists viewed medical and psychiatric portrayals of homosexuality to be just as problematic as the religious views.*[21]

---

20. Fred Fejes, *Gay Rights and Moral Panic: The Origins of America's Debate on Homosexuality* (New York, NY: Palgrave Macmillan, 2008), 33.

21. "The History of Psychiatry & Homosexuality," *LGBT Mental Health Syllabus,* 2012, http://aglp.org/gap/1_history/.

This newer view was exemplified by prominent gay activist Frank Kameny when he said, "Psychiatry is the enemy incarnate. Psychiatry has waged a relentless war of extermination against us. You may take this as a declaration of war against you."[22]

In 1970 and 1971, gay activists picketed and disrupted the American Psychiatric Association meetings in forceful attempts to get the group to change its stance on homosexuality. In 1972, a special panel at the APA's annual meeting was entitled "Psychiatry: Friend or Foe to Homosexuals: A Dialogue." This panel consisted of gay activists Barbara Gittings and Frank Kameny, as well as masked psychiatrist "Dr. Anonymous" (later revealed to be Dr. John E. Fryer), a gay man who spoke on the fears of losing his position as a certified psychiatrist if his colleagues knew the truth about his sexuality. The theatrics and political maneuvering paid off, and in 1973 the Board of Trustees of the American Psychiatric Association voted to remove homosexuality from the *DSM*—no longer classifying it as a mental disorder.

In his history of these events, Ronald Bayer summarizes the redefinition of homosexuality by the APA this way:

*The entire process, from the first confrontations organized by gay demonstrators at psychiatric conventions to the referendum demanded by orthodox psychiatrists, seemed to violate the most basic expectations about how questions of science should be resolved. Instead of being engaged in a sober consideration*

22. *The Advocate*, May 26, 1971, 3. Cited in Ronald Bayer, *Homosexuality and American Psychiatry: The Politics of Diagnosis* (Princeton, NJ: Princeton University Press, 1987), 105.

*of data, psychiatrists were swept up in a political controversy.
The American Psychiatric Association had fallen victim to
the disorder of a tumultuous era, when disruptive conflicts
threatened to politicize every aspect of American social life. . . .
The result was not a conclusion based on an approximation
of the scientific truth as dictated by reason, but was instead
an action demanded by the ideological temper of the times.*[23]

This landmark decision led to a decisive shift in cultural
attitudes about homosexuality. Other mental health groups
such as the American Psychological Association followed
suit in "depathologizing" homosexuality within their own
literature. Activists began citing the 1973 American Psychiatric Association decision as scientific proof that homosexuality was healthy and normal, lobbying for their causes in
other arenas. Even the word *gay*—which had once meant
"happy" or "carefree"—was becoming the preferred terminology. *Gay* was less focused on sex and seemed to express
joy in romance and attraction, whereas the word *homosexual*
was forever tied to the psychiatric history of mental illness.
*Sexual orientation* was now being seen as an essential aspect
of a person—something that should be accepted rather than
resisted. Nevertheless, there were many medical professionals who disagreed with this forced change of direction.

The growth of *reparative therapy* was a way of addressing
the many men and women with unwanted same-sex attractions who now felt abandoned by the psychiatric and psychological establishments. While there were many "ex-gay"

---

23. Ronald Bayer, *Homosexuality and American Psychiatry: The Politics of Diagnosis*
(Princeton, NJ: Princeton University Press, 1987), 3–4.

ministries that provided religious counseling surrounding same-sex attraction (including many that were under the umbrella organization Exodus International), Drs. Joseph Nicolosi, Benjamin Kaufman, and Charles Socarides created a secular treatment alternative with the establishment of the National Association for the Research and Therapy of Homosexuality (NARTH) in 1992. According to cofounder Benjamin Kaufman:

*NARTH came into existence in response to threats to take away the right of patients to choose therapy to eliminate or lessen same-sex attraction. NARTH defends the right of therapists to provide such treatment and provides a forum for the dissemination of research on homosexuality.*[24]

Reparative therapy became a controversial topic as activists focused their attention on discrediting the practice, and the American Psychiatric Association released official position statements against it in 1998 and 2000. While the APA admitted there wasn't enough data to conclusively say whether the practice was effective or harmful, it also asserted that reparative therapists were promoting an oppressive ideology: "In the current social climate, claiming homosexuality is a mental disorder stems from efforts to discredit the growing social acceptance of homosexuality as a normal variant of human sexuality."[25] In response to the

---

24. Benjamin Kaufman, "Why NARTH? The American Psychiatric Association's Destructive and Blind Pursuit of Political Correctness," *Regent University Law Review* 14, no. 2 (2001–2002): 423, https://regentparents.regent.edu/acad/schlaw/student_life/studentorgs/lawreview/docs/issues/v14n2/Vol.%2014,%20No.%202,%207%20Kaufman.pdf.

25. "Position Statement 200001: Therapies Focused on Attempts to Change

vehement push against reparative therapy by mental health organizations, psychologist Dr. Nicholas Cummings said, "'Homophobia as intimidation' is one of the most pervasive techniques used to silence anyone who would disagree with the gay activist agenda."[26]

As activists targeted what was now frequently called *conversion therapy*, mental health groups that had once been ambivalent toward or lightly dismissive of the practice were now quickly joining the chorus of outright derision. By 2009, this is how the American Psychological Association spoke of sexual orientation change efforts:

> *The American Psychological Association advises parents, guardians, young people, and their families to avoid sexual orientation change efforts that portray homosexuality as a mental illness or developmental disorder and to seek psycho-therapy, social support and educational services that provide accurate information on sexual orientation and sexuality, increase family and school support, and reduce rejection of sexual minority youth.*[27]

---

Sexual Orientation (Reparative or Conversion Therapies)," American Psychiatric Association, March 2000, web archive snapshot from January 11, 2012: https://web.archive.org/web/20120111072832/http://www.psych.org/Departments/EDU/Library/APAOfficialDocumentsandRelated/PositionStatements/200001.aspx.

26. Linda Ames Nicolosi, "Psychology Losing Credibility, Says APA Insiders," National Association for the Research and Treatment of Homosexuality, web archive snapshot from March 11, 2012, https://web.archive.org/web/20120311233215/http://www.narth.com/docs/insiders.html.

27. Glassgold, Judith M., et al. *Report of the American Psychological Association Task Force on Appropriate Therapeutic Responses to Sexual Orientation* (Washington, DC: American Psychological Association, 2009), 121, https://www.apa.org/pi/lgbt/resources/therapeutic-response.pdf.

Despite no clear scientific consensus on the causes of homosexuality, scientists were absolutely certain that reparative therapy was based on wrong assumptions about its origins and should be replaced with more "affirmative" treatments.

Throughout these years, a differentiation was increasingly made between *sexual orientation* (defined as a pattern of sexual and romantic attractions for people of the same or opposite sex) and *sexual identity* (defined as self-awareness of one's sexual orientation and the private and public ways of identifying with it).[28] The job of mental health providers, therefore, was to help clients find congruence between their sexual orientation and their sexual identity by removing internalized stigma and shame. This meant helping clients accept their sexual orientation as healthy and helping them develop a sexual identity that felt true for them. As theories of identity within social groups increased in the public consciousness, *sexual identity* became enshrined as an essential standpoint from which to view and understand society.

This is where we find ourselves today.

---

28. Ibid., 30.

# Born That Way?

*Homosexuality is not a choice. It is an orientation. It is no different than eye-color, or being right-handed or left-handed. My sexuality is a gift from God and I believe that he intends for me to rejoice in that by knowing the love of another in a life-time, monogamous relationship.* — Anonymous Gay Christian, a letter to the CEO of Chick-fil-A[29]

As homosexuality has become socially normalized, it has been common for people to argue that sexual orientation is inborn—implying a genetic origin. Some theories considered the size of the hypothalamus, overexposure to certain hormones during fetal gestation, or even a specific "gay gene" as potential causes for homosexuality. These theories have all been debunked.

More recently, a 2019 study analyzed DNA samples and lifestyle information from 470,000 people (the largest such study to date) and found "no clear patterns among genetic variants that could be used to meaningfully predict or identify a person's sexual behavior."[30] This study indicates that "non-genetic factors—such as cultural environment, upbringing, personality, nurturing—are far more significant in influencing a person's choice of sexual partner."[31]

---

29. "Letter from a Gay Christian," Room for All, August 3, 2012, https://roomforall.com/dt_testimonials/letter-from-a-gay-christian/.

30. Kate Kelland, "No 'Gay Gene,' but Study Finds Genetic Links to Sexual Behavior," Reuters, August 29, 2019, https://www.reuters.com/article/us-science-sex/no-gay-gene-but-study-finds-genetic-links-to-sexual-behavior-idUSKCN1VJ2C3.

31. Ibid.

After an extensive look into the medical data concerning homosexuality in 2016, psychiatrists Lawrence S. Mayer and Paul R. McHugh offered their critique of the popular "born that way" notion:

*Some of the most widely held views about sexual orientation, such as the 'born that way' hypothesis, simply are not supported by science. The literature in this area does describe a small ensemble of biological differences between non-heterosexuals and heterosexuals, but those biological differences are not sufficient to predict sexual orientation, the ultimate test of any scientific finding.*[32]

This is, of course, nothing new, as even older books that have tried to objectively understand the homosexual phenomenon have recognized the lack of medical data supporting the "born that way" thesis. For example, Alan J. Cooper, Honorary Senior Lecturer in Psychiatry at St. Mary's Hospital Medical School in London, gave an overview of the potential origins of homosexuality. Using genetic data available to him in 1974, he said, "Although data from many sophisticated genetic studies have been recently available the conclusions are far from definitive."[33] He concluded his essay by saying:

---

32. Lawrence S. Mayer and Paul R. McHugh, "Sexuality and Gender: Findings from the Biological, Psychological, and Social Sciences," *The New Atlantis: A Journal of Technology & Society*, Special Report, no. 50 (Fall 2016): 114, https://www.thenewatlantis.com/docLib/20160819_TNA50SexualityandGender.pdf.

33. A. J. Cooper, "The Aetiology of Homosexuality," in *Understanding Homosexuality: Its Biological and Psychological Basis*, ed. J.A. Loraine (Lancaster, England: Medical and Technical Publishing Co., 1974), 5.

*Generally however, it must be conceded that in spite of a great deal of work and many ingenious theories the causes of homosexuality remain undetermined. It may well be that the complexity of society will defeat all investigative efforts and keep it this way.*[34]

Despite the longstanding results of this research, the idea of a biological cause has had tremendous political value. John D'Emilio, gay activist and gender studies professor at the University of Illinois at Chicago, explains:

*"Born gay" is an idea with a large constituency, LGBT and otherwise. It's an idea designed to allay the ingrained fears of a homophobic society and the internalized fears of gays, lesbians, and bisexuals. What's most amazing to me about the "born gay" phenomenon is that the scientific evidence for it is thin as a reed, yet it doesn't matter. It's an idea with such social utility that one doesn't need much evidence in order to make it attractive and credible.*[35]

Lesbian feminist Camille Paglia offers a similar take:

*Nature exists, whether academics like it or not. And in nature, procreation is the single, relentless rule. That is the norm. Our sexual bodies were designed for reproduction. Penis fits vagina: no fancy linguistic game-playing can change that biologic fact. . . . No one is "born gay." The idea is ridiculous,*

---

34. Ibid., 21.

35. John D'Emilio, "LGBT Liberation: Build a Broad Movement," interview by Sherry Wolf, *International Socialist Review*, Issue #65, May–June 2009, https://isreview.org/issue/65/lgbt-liberation-build-broad-movement.

*but it is symptomatic of our over-politicized climate that such assertions are given instant credence by gay activists and their media partisans.*[36]

Nevertheless, many researchers believe that "positive attitudes toward homosexuality are associated with the belief that its origins are biological, whereas negative attitudes are associated with the view that its origin is personal choice."[37] So the narrative continues. Political organizations carefully adjust their language to imply a biological origin without explicitly stating it. For instance, the LGBT advocacy group the Human Rights Campaign defines sexual orientation as "an inherent or immutable enduring emotional, romantic or sexual attraction to other people."[38] The word *inherent* implies biological origin but gives plausible deniability if questioned.

In "gay Christian" circles, the "born that way" argument takes on an added theological dimension when some "gay Christians" want to say that their homosexual orientation is a unique aspect of how God made them. Former United Methodist pastor Jimmy Creech says:

*How do I view God's position on "homosexuality?" I believe lesbian, gay and bisexual people to be a part of God's wondrous creation, created to be just who they are, and completely loved*

36. Camille Paglia, *Vamps & Tramps: New Essays* (New York: Vintage Books, 1994), 70–71.

37. Jane P. Sheldon et al., "Beliefs about the Etiology of Homosexuality and about the Ramifications of Discovering Its Possible Genetic Origin," *Journal of Homosexuality* 52 (2007): 111–150, https://www.ncbi.nlm.nih.gov/pmc/articles/PMC4545255/.

38. "Sexual Orientation and Gender Identity Definitions," Human Rights Campaign, accessed August 9, 2021, https://www.hrc.org/resources/sexual-orientation-and-gender-identity-terminology-and-definitions.

*and treasured by God. I believe God does not intend for anyone to be alone but to live in companionship. And I believe God expects healthy loving relationships to include sexual love. The Bible doesn't say this, of course. But neither does it deny it. I believe this to be true not only because of the Bible's emphasis on the goodness of God's creation and the supreme value of love, but because of the greater understanding of human nature that we have available to us today. I do not believe that God intends us to live in the small world of ancient biblical culture, but rather in God's larger evolving world informed by science, reason and experience.* [39]

Malcolm Boyd went even further, offering a liturgical reading for congregations to speak over their LGBT congregants: "We offer you validation for yourself as you have been created and celebration of your gayness as a gift of God."[40]

Progressive Christians readily embraced the language of *sexual orientation*, while conservative Christians maintained ambivalence or even resistance to the term. Many saw it as a capitulation to the assault of secular science on the Christian worldview—removing moral culpability from homosexual sin altogether. However, as activists demanded that reparative therapy be criminalized, debates in conservative circles shifted in the 2010s. Concerned about the impact of their sexual ethics on their public witness, conservative Christians

39. "What the Bible Says about Homosexuality. What the Bible Says about Marriage." Human Rights Campaign, web archive snapshot from June 24, 2020, https://web.archive.org/web/20200624201309/https://www.hrc.org/resources/what-does-the-bible-say-about-homosexuality/.

40. Kitteridge Cherry, "Spiritual Resources Honor National Coming Out Day," *Q Spirit*, October 11, 2019, https://qspirit.net/national-coming-out-day/.

suddenly began to rethink their resistance to the concept of sexual orientation and add nuance to their position on it. One notable example of this was Albert Mohler—stalwart conservative commentator and president of Southern Baptist Theological Seminary—who, at a 2014 conference, announced that he "repented" of denying sexual orientation.

Mohler explained in an essay after the conference:

*I had previously denied the existence of sexual orientation. I, along with many other evangelicals, did so because we did not want to accept the sexual identity structure that so often goes with sexual orientation. I still reject that notion of sexual identity. But I repented of denying the existence of sexual orientation because denying it was deeply confusing to people struggling with same-sex attraction. Biblical Christians properly resist any suggestion that our will can be totally separated from sexual desire, but we really do understand that the will is not a sufficient explanation for a pattern of sexual attraction. Put simply, most people experiencing a same-sex attraction tell of discovering it within themselves at a very early age, certainly within early puberty. As they experience it, a sexual attraction or interest simply "happens," and they come to know it. . . . The concept of sexual orientation is not only helpful, it is in some sense essential. Even those who argue against its existence have to describe and affirm something tantamount to it.*[41]

---

41. R. Albert Mohler, "Sexual Orientation and the Gospel of Jesus Christ," November 13, 2014, https://albertmohler.com/2014/11/13/sexual-orientation-and-the-gospel-of-jesus-christ.

In Mohler's explanation, the denial of sexual orientation needed to be rejected by Christians because it wasn't reflective of the experiences of homosexuals. He further argued that because, according to scripture, humans were born with a sin nature, sexual orientation could be understood simply as a reflection of that. He then could make the case against reparative therapy by saying, "Our biblically-informed understanding of sexual orientation will chasten us from having any confidence that there is any rescue from same-sex attraction to be found in any secular approach, therapy, or treatment."[42] What came first: Mohler's updated position on sexual orientation or the scriptural argument that he used to justify the shift? The confusing ambiguity of Mohler's response implies the former.

As many Christians have noted, the language of sexual orientation speaks of an innate and immutable part of a person's being—despite the inability of science to place sexual orientation anywhere outside a person's individual psyche. It is not inherited, as other biological traits may be, nor is it passed on. It is not identifiable through blood tests or brain scans. It can only be determined by what a person says—which is why the psychiatric and psychological establishments have been essential components of gay activism.

*Sexual orientation* also implies—as secular theorists have argued—that keeping people from being able to fully live out their homosexuality is abusive and cruel. This is the logic being used to force Christians to accept gay rights legislation, to solemnize gay marriage, to outlaw conversion therapy, and to silence conservatives from speaking against the cultural

---

42. Ibid.

shifts happening around them. Christians have been right to be skeptical of it. The language of orientation also carves out an area that the Bible doesn't seem to address as deeply: the idea that people can be gay whether or not they ever engage in homosexual intercourse.

## The Rise of "Gay Celibate Christianity"

*A sexual orientation is such a complex and, in most cases, it seems, intractable thing; I for one cannot imagine what "healing" from my orientation would look like, given that it seems to manifest itself not only in physical attraction to male bodies but also in a preference for male company, with all that it entails.* — Wesley Hill, gay celibate theologian[43]

There is a growing trend of theological conservatives embracing the concept of sexual orientation. This group is led by many younger church members who grew up in conservative environments, discovered they were same-sex attracted, and have tried to find alignment between conservative theology and their orientation. Most claim to have tried to change their attractions but were unable to do so. This inability to change is foundational to their acceptance of their homosexual orientation as normal. However, in contrast to open and affirming "gay Christians," "gay celibate Christians" accept that they will not be able to seek sexual

---

43. Wesley Hill, "Is Being Gay Sanctifiable?" Spiritual Friendship: Musings on God, Sexuality, Relationships, February 26, 2014, https://spiritualfriendship.org/2014/02/26/is-being-gay-sanctifiable/.

fulfillment in anything other than natural marriage. Nevertheless, even for those "gay Christians" who claim to uphold the biblical sexual ethics we discussed in chapter 2, homosexuality is innate and immutable.

This can be seen in the foreword to *Costly Obedience: What We Can Learn from the Celibate Gay Christian Community* (2019), where Wesley Hill says that for gay celibate Christians:

> *Acknowledging the permanence of a same-sex sexual orientation didn't involve any shift in Christian moral convictions. These lesbian and gay believers continued to hold to Christianity's historic prohibition of gay sex and began to talk about what it might look like to embrace celibacy and maybe even flourish in it.*[44]

The idea that there is no shift in "Christian moral convictions" by embracing the APA view of sexual orientation has caused controversy in some conservative churches. "Gay celibate Christians" argue that this controversy is mostly the result of homophobia in the church and the stigma that continues to surround the topic of homosexuality. Conservative critics point out that redefining the nature of sin and temptation to the point of being identified by one's central temptation is counter to every command and example we have in scripture. Nevertheless, to many Christians tired of the polarized cultural debate, this idea of immutable

---

44. Wesley Hill, foreword to *Costly Obedience: What We Can Learn from the Celibate Gay Christian Community* by Mark Yarhouse and Olya Zaporozhets (Grand Rapids, MI: Zondervan, 2019), 12–13.

homosexuality and committed celibacy has seemed to be a workable middle ground.

"Gay celibate Christian" author Gregory Coles writes:

> *Is it too dangerous, too unorthodox, to believe that I am uniquely designed to reflect the glory of God? That my orientation, before the fall, was meant to be a gift in appreciating the beauty of my own sex as I celebrated the friendship of the opposite sex? That perhaps within God's flawless original design there might have been eunuchs, people called to lives of holy singleness? We in the church recoil from the word* gay, *from the very notion of same-sex orientation, because we know what it looks like only outside of Eden, where everything has gone wrong. But what if there's goodness hiding within the ruins? What if the calling to gay Christian celibacy is more than just a failure of straightness? What if God dreamed it for me, wove it into the fabric of my being as he knit me together and sang life into me?*[45]

Coles's admission is startling for someone who claims to believe the Bible's teaching on sexuality. He poses it as a "thinking out loud" hypothetical, but the implications of his thought strike at the very heart of Christian orthodoxy. The implication is that God tempts people to sin by giving them an unnatural sexual urge that cannot be fulfilled without breaking His own law.

Not every gay celibate Christian is willing to push their thinking that far—at least not while they're trying to be

---

45. Gregory Coles, *Single, Gay, Christian: A Personal Journey of Faith and Sexual Identity* (Downers Grove, IL: Intervarsity Press, 2017), 46–47.

perceived as orthodox. But Coles's conclusion is logical: if sexual orientation is innate and immutable and if there is something redeemable about one's same-sex attraction, then it goes deeper than the Fall and becomes part of God's design. Homosexuality is no longer a "dishonorable passion" but part of being "fearfully and wonderfully made."

Some "gay celibate Christians" have adjusted their language to say that homosexuality is part of *brokenness* that resulted from the Fall in Genesis 3. Some have referred to it more like a *disorder*. Others have spoken of it like a *disability*. Still others reject all three of those ideas but offer no clear alternative description in their place.

This conflicting and vague language often keeps concerned Christians silent because it is impossible to argue against the rhetoric if the position is undefined or the parameters keep shifting. The implication is that this discussion is beyond the average Christian's ability to understand—it's better to keep silent than to be seen as an insensitive fool.

It is also implied that scriptural language is inadequate in helping us understand and talk about sexuality in the twenty-first century. Nate Collins, founder of a ministry for theologically conservative LGBT Christians called Revoice, argues that Christians actually need to look beyond the scriptures to understand sexual orientation better:

> *How is gayness related to the fall? and What does gayness look like when it's redeemed? Christians have traditionally used terms like sin, temptation, and healing to answer these questions, all of which are found in various texts in Scripture. My suspicion, however, is that we could provide more specific,*

*and potentially more meaningful, answers to these questions if we broaden our search for descriptions of gay people's experience beyond terms explicitly found in Scripture. In essence, I'm proposing that we develop a theology of orientation that can flesh out our biblical doctrines of sin, temptation, and healing.*[46]

With statements like these that minimize the sufficiency of the scripture, it is hard not to see "gay celibate Christianity" leading the church away from faithfulness. Though they don't share the affirming theology of their liberal counterparts, "gay celibate Christians" are still pushing Christians to rethink their theological convictions and wording by stretching the bounds of orthodoxy. They have found comradery with the broader gay rights movement and frequently adopt the identity politics of LGBT to critique conservative churches. They have embraced the dual identities of being "gay Christians," "same-sex attracted Christians," or "queer Christians," claiming that this makes them more effective ambassadors of Christ. One gay celibate speaker succinctly summed up the ideology into six words: "The tomb is empty. Closet, too."[47]

---

46. Nate Collins, *All But Invisible: Exploring Identity Questions at the Intersection of Faith, Gender, and Sexuality* (Grand Rapids, MI: Zondervan, 2017), 190.

47. Grant Hartley (@TheGrantHartley), "The tomb is empty. Closet, too," Twitter, November 15, 2019, 5:16 PM, https://twitter.com/TheGrantHartley/status/1195480655636893698.

# Aesthetic Orientation and Spiritual Friendship

*Straight Christians have the ability to love an opposite-sex person through a sexual union that celibate gay Christians forego. But on the other hand, celibate gay Christians have the unique ability to love their same-sex friends with an intensity that might not come naturally to their straight peers. And this is beautiful.* — Bridget Eileen Rivera, celibate lesbian author[48]

"Gay celibate Christians" claim that same-sex attraction is more than simply a desire for gay sex. They say that it can be a longing for intimacy with someone of the same sex that might be experienced as "a desire for nearness, for partnership, for close friendship, rich conversation, and an overall appreciation of beauty."[49] In other words, they are saying that same-sex attraction is not inherently lustful and therefore not inherently sinful. This poses a subtle challenge to the Christian position.

Some "gay celibate Christians" have come to describe this inward pull as *aesthetic orientation*—a term developed by Nate Collins in his book *All But Invisible*. The idea is that we all have an inherent, morally neutral attraction toward certain kinds of beauty—male beauty or female beauty—that shapes

48. Bridget Eileen Rivera, "Gay Attractions Create the Context for More Than Just Sin," Meditations of a Traveling Nun, June 9, 2018, https://www. meditationsofatravelingnun.com/sex-sin-do-not-define-gay-attractions/

49. Julie Rodgers, "Can the Gay Be a Good?" Spiritual Friendship: Musings on God, Sexuality, Relationships, October 23, 2014, https://spiritualfriendship. org/2014/10/23/can-the-gay-be-a-good/.

our sexuality but the roots of which are not sexual. As Collins describes it:

> *Beneath all the erotic desires that characterize how I experience my sexuality, beneath the attractions I may feel to this or that individual, beneath the skipped heartbeat when a specific guy enters a room, or looks at me, or touches my arm—beneath all these things that we usually associate with sexuality—is the simple perception and appreciation of the beauty of another bearer of the divine image.*[50]

"Gay celibate Christians" describe more than aesthetic orientation, however—they also describe a desire for intimate relationships with people of the same sex. In this vein, gay celibate theologian Wesley Hill attempts to desexualize the very concept of sexuality itself:

> *Celibates do not turn a blind eye to their sexuality because their sexuality is not reducible to their desire for genital intimacy. Sexuality, broadly conceived, is perhaps best understood as an affective capacity for relationality, encompassing the drive toward self-giving and reciprocal knowing in non-genital ways.*[51]

Under Hill's definition (which is at odds with both the common usage of the word and common sense), sexuality is

---

50. Nate Collins, *All But Invisible: Exploring Identity Questions at the Intersection of Faith, Gender, and Sexuality* (Grand Rapids, MI: Zondervan, 2017), 304.

51. Wesley Hill, "Washed and Still Waiting: An Evangelical Approach to Homosexuality," *Journal of the Evangelical Theological Society (JETS)*, 59, no. 2 (June 2016): 331, https://www.etsjets.org/files/JETS-PDFs/59/59-2/JETS_59-2_323-338_Hill.pdf.

merely a desire to be close to someone—however that desire might be expressed. In this case, the existence of sex organs is incidental, despite the fact that they define the type of people he wants to be close to.

This lays the groundwork for Hill's vision of *spiritual friendship*—a type of "vowed spiritual siblinghood" whereby two friends (presumably of the same sex) exchange vows and commit themselves before God to always be there for one another, no matter what. Hill says, "Friendship should be like a marriage: for better for worse, for richer for poorer, till death depart. They cannot be separated whom true amity knitteth."[52] Because he sees normal friendship as "non-binding," he proposes this form of "committed, honored, and anchored relationships" as a solution to the problem of lonely same-sex attracted Christians who want intimacy but think it is available to them only in natural marriage.[53]

In an attempt to find biblical grounding, Hill stretches desperately to include David and Jonathan as well as Ruth and Naomi as prime examples of his kind of "vowed" friendship.[54] What he seems to miss with these examples, however, is that these commitments were born out of extraordinary situations. We have already seen in chapter 2 how the covenant between David and Jonathan was tied to David's ascendency

---

52. Wesley Hill, *Spiritual Friendship: Finding Love in the Church as a Celibate Gay Christian* (Grand Rapids, MI: Brazos Press, 2015), 23.

53. Wesley Hill, "Washed and Still Waiting: An Evangelical Approach to Homosexuality." *Journal of the Evangelical Theological Society (JETS)*, 59, no. 2 (June 2016): 333, https://www.etsjets.org/files/JETS-PDFs/59/59-2/JETS_59-2_323-338_Hill.pdf.

54. Jonathan Merritt, "Celibate Gay Christian Leader Urges Faithful to 'Normalize' Committed Friendships," Religion News Service, April 7, 2015, https://religionnews.com/2015/04/07/celibate-gay-christian-leader-urges-faithful-reimagine-friendship/.

to the throne and later his survival as a man hunted. There was love, but there was also a fundamental recognition of God's purposes in removing Saul and raising up David. Additionally, both men were married and had families; in that way, we are already describing something different from what Hill has in mind.

In Ruth and Naomi's case, it was a bond formed by Ruth's determination to continue with her mother-in-law and to be part of the covenant community of Israel (Ruth 1:16–17). As David H. Linden notes in his critique of Hill:

> *This is not a two-person covenant; it is a commitment of I'm-going-with-you, a pledge regarding location, plus an implied resolve to serve. Naomi's people will be her people. Naomi did not ask for such a commitment, and Scripture does not suggest that Naomi said a similar thing back to her.*[55]

After Boaz takes notice of Ruth, we see Naomi encouraging Ruth to pursue a relationship with Boaz and even coaching her in how best to do it (Ruth 3:1–5). Ruth's devotion and loyalty are exemplary—but the focus of the book still centers around the relationship of Ruth and Boaz and the son they bring forth by their marital union (Ruth 4:13–17).

Godly friendship is a great blessing, but this supposed practice of vowed spiritual friendship as a uniquely intimate relationship *in lieu of* natural marriage is unbiblical. As Derek Brown notes:

---

55. David H. Linden, "A Homosexual Reads His Bible," The Aquila Report, January 2, 2020, https://www.theaquilareport.com/a-homosexual-reads-his-bible/.

*Specifically, it is the Lord's Table observed among a community of believers, not public vows between a same-sex couple, that endows friendship with rich significance. In Christ we are brothers and sisters and our sibling bonds are held fast by the Spirit. As we take the bread and the cup these bonds to Christ and to each other are reaffirmed and strengthened, for we are reminded that we all are partakers of grace and the free gift of salvation through the death of God's Son.*[56]

In vows as members of a local church and in regular participation in the Lord's Supper, the people of God are knit together in a local body where we exercise our spiritual gifts (1 Corinthians 12:4–7), display the fruit of the Spirit (Galatians 5:22–24), and stir up one another to love and good deeds (Hebrews 10:24). Yet even in this we are commanded to highly esteem marriage (Hebrews 13:4). All our relationships must maintain a proper order and place within God's design for the family. There is something in the "holding fast to one's wife" aspect of marriage that must be recognized, preserved, and protected within the bounds of chaste, godly friendship—and this is what the concept of spiritual friendship undermines.

Aesthetic orientation is an attempt to justify homosexuality by fundamentally redefining it. While homosexuality may be more than sexual desire, it certainly includes that desire within its necessary implications. Otherwise, we are merely talking about platonic friendship and there is no need to

---

56. Derek Brown, "A Review of Wesley Hill. *Spiritual Friendship: Finding Love in the Church as a Celibate Gay Christian,*" *The Journal for Biblical Manhood & Womanhood,* XX, no. 2 (Fall 2015): 57, https://cbmw.org/wp-content/uploads/2015/11/20.2_Fall_JBMW_Web_Cover.pdf.

define it specifically as "gay," "queer" or "same-sex attracted." If these same-sex desires are truly benign and nonsexual, why is there a need to constantly stipulate that they should not be expressed sexually—as if sexual expression is the expected consummation of the attraction?

Despite the best efforts of gay celibate theologians to desexualize homosexuality, they simply cannot make these desires biblically acceptable. The seventh commandment forbids adultery: "You shall not commit adultery" (Exodus 20:14). With this, we understand that sexually immoral behavior is outlawed, as well as the lustful desire for it. As Jesus said, "But I say to you that everyone who looks at a woman with lustful intent has already committed adultery with her in his heart" (Matthew 5:28). The tenth commandment is also relevant: "You shall not covet your neighbor's wife" (Exodus 20:17). This passage reminds us that there is a way that a man can desire his neighbor's wife that may not be sexual, yet it is also forbidden—it is an expression of discontentment with God's plan, purposes, and providence. It is desiring something that God has not given.

## "Gay Christian" Identity

*While discussions about terminology can be fruitful, we believe they can also cause unnecessary division within the family of God and needless pain for many non-straight Christians. Whether individuals choose "gay" or "same-sex-attracted" to describe their orientation and experience is a matter of wisdom and liberty, and should not divide believers who otherwise share a commitment to historic Christian teaching about marriage and sexuality.* — Revoice, Statement on Sexual Ethics and Christian Obedience[57]

The use of the term *gay Christian* has garnered particular attention from conservatives with the emergence of gay celibate theology. Even Side B proponents are mixed on it. Revoice considers personal terminology a point of Christian liberty, while Living Out generally discourages the use of *gay Christian*. Yet it is insisted that Christians should not be very concerned about what people decide to call themselves. Is *gay* merely a recognition of sinful experience, or is it something akin to an identity label? Is it proper for Christians to describe themselves as *gay Christians*? These are questions that many conservative churches are beginning to ask.

Those who defend the use of *gay Christian* typically say that *gay* doesn't speak to an identity. This is how Preston Sprinkle defends it:

---

57. "Statement on Sexual Ethics and Christian Obedience," Revoice, accessed January 18, 2021, https://revoice.us/about/our-beliefs/statements-of-conviction/statement-on-sexual-ethics-and-christian-obedience/.

*"Gay" doesn't mean gay sex, or gay lust, nor does it have to refer to one's core identity or fundamental essence as a person. "Gay" simply means that someone is attracted to the same sex and not to the opposite sex.*[58]

For Sprinkle, it is appropriate for Christians to describe their experience of homosexual desire with the culturally understood term *gay*. He argues that it is merely a point of clarity—describing people's *sexual orientation*, not their *sexual identity*. Meanwhile, for gay celibate author Gregory Coles, the term *gay* describes his attractions while also pushing against conservative expectations of orientation change: "'Gay' declares without apology the likely permanence of my state during this lifetime and the need for Christian churches to seriously reckon with the presence of people like me in their midst."[59]

Although Sprinkle and Coles speak as if *gay* is just a harmless word describing experience, celibate gay Catholic blogger Chris Damian recognizes its associative power. In fact, that is exactly why he uses it:

*To adopt the term "gay" is to adopt a certain kind of identity, with political, religious, philosophical, and social implications. This is part of why I use the word. To say "I am gay" is*

58. Preston Sprinkle, "Why I Support the Revoice Conference." The Center for Faith, Sexuality & Gender, June 26, 2018, https://centerforfaith.com/blog/why-i-support-the-revoice-conference.

59. Greg Coles, "Three Concerns with the Term 'Same-Sex Attracted,'" The Center for Faith, Sexuality & Gender, February 19, 2019, https://www.centerforfaith.com/blog/three-concerns-with-the-term-same-sex-attracted.

*to say that I am adopting some part of this community, and that I am in some part responsible for it.*[60]

We can assume that Damian likely has several differences of opinion with the political, religious, philosophical, and social worldview of the gay community at large, yet *gay* expresses enough of who he is that he happily takes on the label, whatever else may be attached to it.

In contrast to that, Rachel Gilson, author of *Born Again This Way* (2020), believes the terms *gay* or *lesbian Christian* miscommunicate. "*Lesbian* seemed to carry much more with it than just romantic and sexual attraction. It felt more like a whole outlook, a label that included certain political and social leanings that just didn't feel like me."[61] Sam Allberry, a gay celibate pastor and cofounder of Living Out, also recognizes the problematic nature of a Christian calling himself gay:

*In our secular culture, the language people would typically and obviously use would be to say, "Well, I'm gay." But in my own experience that kind of language tends to be used to express, not just a description of what kind of sexual feelings you have, but it tends (to me) to be someone's identity. It's an indication of who you are.*[62]

---

60. Chris Damian, "Why I Call Myself a 'Gay Catholic,'" January 5, 2018, https://chrisdamian.net/2018/01/05/why-i-call-myself-a-gay-catholic/.

61. Rachel Gilson, "Why I Started Calling Myself Same-Sex Attracted," The Center for Faith, Sexuality & Gender, February 15, 2019, https://www.centerforfaith.com/blog/why-i-started-calling-myself-same-sex-attracted.

62. Sam Allberry, "The Christian Debate over Sexual Identity," Desiring God, July 13, 2018, https://www.desiringgod.org/interviews/the-christian-debate-over-sexual-identity.

This is why Rachel Gilson and Sam Allberry refer to themselves as *same-sex attracted Christians*, even though the nuance is slight and the new term still poses similar problems as *gay Christian*.

People may be very specific in their language and may have deeply personal reasons for the labels they have chosen. Yet how long before these labels feel insufficient? For instance, a 2019 Bustle editorial speaks of a growing number of people who find it "burdensome" or even "impossible" to find a category that fits their particular orientation. The author even gives four reasons why someone might avoid sexual identity labels: "1) Sexual orientation is a social construct, 2) sexual orientation is not clear-cut, 3) these labels are hard to apply to me as a non-binary person, 4) you never know who you'll be attracted to."[63] Such is the burden of highly individualized language.

The reality is that it is impossible to separate the use of personal terminology from the bigger question of *sexual identity*. In fact, when someone "comes out as gay," we would say they *identify as gay* rather than they *describe themselves as gay*. That's because *gay* is recognized as an *identity label*.[64] No one denies that *gay* includes a description of attractions, but the act of "coming out" is itself a public identification. Psychologists such as Side B proponent Mark Yarhouse describe the "adoption of a private or public sexual identity label, such

---

63. Suzannah Weiss, "4 Reasons I Don't Label My Sexual Orientation—And You Don't Have to Either," Bustle, June 11, 2019, https://www.bustle.com/p/why-sexual-orientation-labels-arent-for-me-you-dont-have-to-use-them-either-17990747.

64. Arielle E. White et al. "Gender Identity and Sexual Identity Labels Used by U.S. High School Students: A Co-occurrence Network Analysis." *Psychology of Sexual Orientation and Gender Diversity*, 5, no. 2 (2018), https://doi.org/10.1037/sgd0000266.

as 'gay'" as an important milestone in the development of sexual identity, further proof that these things are inextricably tied together.[65]

This is where Sam Allberry's term *same-sex attracted Christian* still falls short. While Allberry rightly teaches that a Christian's identity is given by God—not discovered in us or created by us—he attempts to draw an implied distinction between our *spiritual identity* and our *sexual identity*. In this view, the spiritual identity is clearly defined by scripture while the sexual identity is left to be discovered by us—which means it is ultimately defined by personal experience. In this way, the Bible becomes a mere guide to good behavior, moderating how we live, rather than God's intentions and directives for humanity that ultimately define us.

Scripture doesn't give us any unique *sexual identities* outside of *men* and *women*—identities that are given to us by God at conception. Sexual intercourse is meant only for a husband and wife in marriage, bringing together two naturally distinct image bearers of God in covenant union with one another. Where the Bible may describe other "sexual identities," they are violations of God's law and God's design—adulterers, fornicators, prostitutes, homosexuals, sexually immoral. Our sexual identity is intrinsically tied to our biological sex. A man cannot become a *wife* and a woman cannot become a *husband*. Those terms are sex-specific, and they are not fair game for redefinition.

Whatever a person feels "deep down" is not representative of ultimate reality. A person may be frequently tempted

---

65. Mark Yarhouse and Olya Zaporozhets. *Costly Obedience: What We Can Learn from the Celibate Gay Christian Community* (Grand Rapids, MI: Zondervan, 2019), 114.

by homosexual lust, but is that person, essentially, a homosexual? Theologian R.C. Sproul would say no. Rather, on this subject he advocated that Christians recognize that "biologically, essentially, and intrinsically, there is no such thing as a homosexual."[66] His reason for arguing this wasn't to denigrate a person's experience but to highlight that our understanding of reality needs to be grounded by the Bible. He recognized that a wrong *self-conception* (what a person believes about himself) was behind so much of the sexual confusion happening in our world, locking people into a way of seeing themselves that keeps them in bondage to their own sinful desires and behaviors. It is a radical rebuke to our psychologically fixated world that chafes against the yoke of God's definitions.

How we think about ourselves matters. It has implications for what we do, people we listen to, ideas we embrace, and counsel we give. The Bible does speak to questions of identity, but it doesn't speak the way the world does. When we read Genesis 1, we learn that human beings are created in the image of God; when we read Genesis 3, we learn that human beings sinned against God. When we read Romans 3, we see that "all have sinned and fall short of the glory of God" (Romans 3:23), and when we read Romans 5, we see that there are only two camps—those who are "in Adam" and those who are "in Christ."

We naturally have other labels that describe our roles in the home or society. The Bible recognizes this too. We read commands to fathers and mothers, to children, to slaves

---

66. R. C. Sproul, "Homosexuality," Ligonier Ministries, accessed August 9, 2021, https://www.ligonier.org/learn/series/homosexuality/.

and masters, to old women and young women, old men and young men. There are all kinds of identity markers throughout the pages of scripture. Sometimes they are descriptive, and sometimes they tie in deeply to our own self-worth and sense of purpose. These distinctions used to be commonly understood and are not based on personal feeling.

The Bible does not treat our use of language lightly: "If anyone thinks he is religious and does not bridle his tongue but deceives his heart, this person's religion is worthless" (James 1:26). Nor does it indicate that our language is merely a neutral form of personal expression: "And the tongue is a fire, a world of unrighteousness. The tongue is set among our members, staining the whole body, setting on fire the entire course of life, and set on fire by hell" (James 3:6).

Language informs and gives categories to our thinking. When we stray from biblical language and biblical categories, we will inevitably stray from biblical truth. It is no coincidence that the broader LGBT movement has presented an assault on language, constantly redefining terms and demanding adherence to new terminology.[67] Likewise, "gay Christianity" offers its own reformulation of language and, in some cases, so deeply personalizes its expression to the point that it fails to communicate clearly.

It should be noted that the debate over "gay Christian" terminology is primarily a debate between conservative churches and proponents of gay celibate theology. Gay-affirming Christians and other theological progressives do not

---

67. Kaz Weida, "LGBTQIA+Everyone: The State of Inclusive Language around the World," *Rosetta Stone* (blog), June 26, 2020, https://blog.rosettastone.com/lgbtqeveryone-the-state-of-inclusive-language-around-the-world/.

struggle with the term *gay Christian* because it just seems normal and expected. To them, if a person identifies as gay and as a Christian, then that person obviously a "gay Christian."

If we're being honest, we must recognize that the term *gay Christian* embraces two identity markers: *gay* by fundamental experience and *Christian* by professed conviction. Some people might say to be gay is even more fundamental to who they are because they didn't choose it and can't change it. Contrast that with how 2 Corinthians 5:17 describes believers: "Therefore, if anyone is in Christ, he is a new creation. The old has passed away; behold, the new has come."

Some have come back and said that Paul identifies himself as a sinner, so it is not inappropriate to identify as someone marred and broken by sin. But notice that when Paul identifies as a sinner, it is in the context of repentance. That struggle with indwelling sin as a believer—most clearly articulated in Romans 7—leads Paul to cry out, "Wretched man that I am! Who will deliver me from this body of death?" (Romans 7:24). That is not the heart cry of someone who embraces their identity as a sinner.

If a person were to say, "I'm a porn-addicted Christian" or "I'm a covetous Christian, and I can't change my desires," we would immediately have questions about their sanctification or even their profession of faith. And we should. Of course, such statements seem outlandish because no one is trying to publicly hold those sins up as matters of personal identity. But homosexuality is treated differently.

*Gay Christian* is rightly controversial because faithful Christians can immediately see what is being implied by it. Do "gay Christians" hate their sin, or do they relish in it as if it's a unique badge of honor? The Chris Damian quote that opened this section cuts through some of the double-speak and gets to the heart of the matter—to embrace a "gay Christian" label is to embrace a "gay" identity. It may seem as if terminology and identity are separate issues, but in reality, they are inextricably tied together.

## What's the Problem?

*Put to death therefore what is earthly in you: sexual immoral-ity, impurity, passion, evil desire, and covetousness, which is idolatry. On account of these the wrath of God is coming.*
— Colossians 3:5–6

We are left with the question of sexual orientation. Is the Bible concerned only with homosexual intercourse, or is same-sex attraction sinful in itself? There is no denying that the Bible's language surrounding homosexuality focuses primarily on homosexual intercourse, yet we would be foolish to assume that the Bible is silent on matters of the heart—including lust, wrongful attractions, and covetousness.

We have already seen in chapter 2 how Christ sees sins of the heart as equally sinful before God. They must be repented of and mortified (Romans 8:13). We also have seen that homosexual intercourse is, according to Paul, unnatural and shameful. It is something that should be plainly seen as sinful. If these are Paul's words for the behavior, why would desiring the behavior be acceptable? Why would building an identity that is shaped by the influence of those who indulge the flesh be acceptable? If we carve out space in our thinking that allows for the cultivation of one sinful desire (even one we claim we will never act on), are we truly submitted to the Lordship of Christ?

Let's return to Romans 1:26 for a moment. "For this reason God gave them up to dishonorable passions. For their women exchanged natural relations for those that are contrary to nature." While this passage clearly describes the sinfulness of homosexual behavior, the phrase "dishonorable passions" (or "degrading passions") indicates that homosexual attraction is, in itself, sinful. *Pathos* (πάθος), the word used here in the plural for "passions," describes the "experience of strong desire."[68] The description of these passions as *passions "of dishonor"* (ἀτιμίας | *atimias*) underscores their sinful, degrading nature. They bring moral shame on the person indulging in them.[69] Therefore, this phrase describes a sinful mental disposition that is the first step toward immoral behavior. The God who restrains evil gave these people over to the evil that they so passionately desired. There is something disordered in the thinking of those who indulge in "dishonorable passions" that leads to disordered behavior.

The word *pathos* ("passion") pops up again in Colossians 3:5, cited above: "Put to death therefore what is earthly in you: sexual immorality, impurity, passion, evil desire, and covetousness, which is idolatry." By linking "sexual immorality" with "impurity, passion, evil desire, covetousness," and "idolatry," Paul emphasizes the sinfulness of sexually immoral

---

68. Frederick William Danker, ed., *A Greek-English Lexicon of the New Testament and Other Early Christian Literature*, 3rd ed. (Chicago and London: University of Chicago Press, 2000), s. v. πάθος.

69. Ibid., s.v. ἀτιμία.

desires as well as sexually immoral acts. The implications of the terms are important, so let's take a moment to consider each of them.

**Sexual immorality** (πορνεία | *porneia*): illicit sexual intercourse; a broad category of sexual behavior that includes adultery, fornication, homosexuality, bestiality, incest, and any other conceivable illicit sexual act.[70]

**Impurity** (ἀκαθαρσία | *akatharsia*): uncleanness; "immorality, vileness" especially in reference to sexual sins. In Romans 1:24 and Ephesians 5:3, this word refers to "unnatural vices."[71] By associating this term with other words denoting sexual immorality, Paul emphasizes the moral uncleanness of illicit sexual desires as well as behavior. This word also describes the uncleanness of lustful, reckless, extravagant living.[72]

**Passion** (πάθος | *pathos*): as mentioned above, the "experience of strong desire, passion."[73] It is a feeling which the mind suffers, an affection of the mind, emotion, passion, passionate desire.[74] This term gets at the roots of desire, especially desires for that which God has forbidden.

**Evil desire** (κακή ἐπιθυμία | *kakē epithymia*): *Evil* (*kakē*) may imply the harmful nature of these passions as well as

---

70. Ibid., s.v. πορνεία.

71. Ibid., s.v. ἀκαθαρσία.

72. *Thayer's Greek Lexicon*, Electronic Database, "Lexicon: Strong's G167 – akatharsia." Biblesoft Inc.

73. Frederick William Danker, ed., *A Greek-English Lexicon of the New Testament and Other Early Christian Literature*, 3rd ed. (Chicago and London: University of Chicago Press, 2000), s.v. πάθος.

74. *Thayer's Greek Lexicon, Electronic Database, "Lexicon: Strong's G3806 – pathos."* Biblesoft Inc.

their moral sinfulness.[75] *Desire* (*Epithymia*) often, as here, describes "desire for what is forbidden," "craving, lust."[76] The fact that Paul combines *evil* with the word for "lust" testifies to how seriously God views the sin of lust and how easily seemingly benign desire can lead to wickedness.

**Covetousness** (πλεονεξία | *pleonexia*): "greediness, insatiableness, avarice."[77] While it is sometimes used to refer to greediness for material gain (Luke 12:15, 2 Peter 2:3), its use in Colossians 3 is similar to the way it is used in Ephesians 4:19: "They have become callous and have given themselves up to sensuality, *greedy* to practice every kind of impurity" (emphasis mine).

**Idolatry** (εἰδωλολατρία | *eidōlolatria*): the worship of false gods.[78] Ultimately, Paul sees the embracing of covetousness as an expression of idolatry rather than the other way around, indicating that idolatry is a sin of the heart and is something that gives birth to other sins.

The language is emphatic, clear, and all-inclusive of anything that might be tied to the fruits or roots of sexual sin. These things must be put to death in every believer's heart. In fact, it is because of these things that the wrath of God is coming (Colossians 3:6). We have put off the old self and have put on the new self, "which is being renewed in knowledge after the image of its creator" (Colossians 3:10).

---

75. κακή is the feminine form of the adjective κακός—in order to agree with ἐπιθυμία. Frederick William Danker, ed., *A Greek-English Lexicon of the New Testament and Other Early Christian Literature*, 3rd ed. (Chicago and London: University of Chicago Press, 2000), s.v. κακός.

76. Ibid., s.v. ἐπιθυμία.

77. Ibid., s.v. πλεονεξία.

78. *Thayer's Greek Lexicon*, Electronic Database. "Lexicon: Strong's G1495 – eidololatria." Biblesoft Inc.

The call of being renewed in knowledge is every believer's task. It is the task of the young man who wants to secretly indulge in pornography and satisfies his guilt by thinking this is just his "thorn in the flesh," or the woman who cannot wait to gossip about the person who has hurt her feelings because "they really deserve it," or the child who wishes his restrictive parents were more like his friend's looser parents. Our minds are breeding grounds for all manner of sin. This is why Paul warns us not to be conformed to this world's way of thinking and behaving but to be transformed by the renewal of our minds (Romans 12:2). If the Holy Spirit indwells us because we are truly God's children, then our striving is not in vain. We will overcome, and our thinking will change.

As Christians, our relationship to sin has changed because we are now under the lordship of Jesus Christ (Romans 6:1–4). Sin is no longer something that rules us but something we can (and increasingly do) overcome (Romans 6:22). But in order to put sin to death, we must deal with our thought life. Paul exhorts us in Romans:

*So you also must consider yourselves dead to sin and alive to God in Christ Jesus. Let not sin therefore reign in your mortal body, to make you obey its passions. Do not present your members to sin as instruments for unrighteousness, but present yourselves to God as those who have been brought from death to life, and your members to God as instruments for righteousness. For sin will have no dominion over you, since you are not under law but under grace.* (Romans 6:11–14)

This is a word of conviction and encouragement to the homosexual struggler. Do not be defined by your temptation. Do not submit yourself to the lusts of your mind. Do not keep yourself from the Holy Spirit's conviction by saying you were born this way and will always remain this way. There are a thousand voices wanting you to look inward and self-actualize based on your feelings. In the heat of the struggle against the flesh, it is tempting to think the struggle is ultimate reality. But scripture points us to something objectively true of even the most feeble and frail believer: we are dead to sin and alive to God. This objective reality enables us to resist sin and to put it to death.

Many claim that change is impossible, and they resist any notion that a person can find freedom from homosexual identity and lust. Despite these claims, many Christians have submitted themselves to God and found freedom and healing from their lusts—in body, mind, and soul. One example of this is First Stone Ministries in Oklahoma City. Their website is full of credible testimonies of men and women who have renewed (and continue to renew) their minds by the Word of God, under the power of the Holy Spirit.[79] Rather than buying into the lie that homosexuality is inborn, we should all see ourselves as God intends for us to be and strive to live in accordance with His design and plan.

True children of God should know that they cannot make these allowances for sin and that if they do, their conscience will be tormented by the Holy Spirit's conviction until they repent. As Richard F. Lovelace recognized

---

79. First Stone Ministries, https://www.firststone.org.

in 1978 (before these debates over sexual identity had fully materialized):

> *The attempt to persuade the conscience that homosexuality is sinful only if it is expressed in outward acts will not pacify the conscience, which grasps instinctively the fact that all inner motives which are not perfectly channeled according to the will of God are sin. The homosexual Christian must therefore learn to relax in the honest admission that his motives are disordered, but he must commit himself to their reordering— or at least restraint—through the power of Christ infused in the process of sanctification. As he exercises the faith to believe that he is accepted [by God because of Christ], he must also face the harder task of believing that he is free not to act out the compulsive drives that still may inhere in a part of his personality.*[80]

Is homosexual sin different from heterosexual sin? In the sense of earning God's judgment, no—all sin is equal to condemn us. But there is a different character to homosexual sin in light of creation. Because homosexual desire has no proper fulfilment in God's design for creation, it can rightly be called (as some theologians have) a *disordered desire*. Paul calls it unnatural. In that way it is different from a man lusting after a woman in that men and women were made to find sexual complementarity and fulfillment in each other within the marriage union. Paul could not rightly tell two young men who burn with passion for each other, "It

---

80. Richard F. Lovelace, *Homosexuality and the Church: Crisis, Conflict, Compassion* (Old Tappan, NJ: Fleming H. Revell Company, 1978), 135–136.

is better to marry than burn with passion" (1 Corinthians 7:9), because homosexual intercourse is an abomination and Christian marriage is decidedly heterosexual in its makeup as founded in creation.

In his commentary on Romans, Presbyterian theologian John Murray discusses the unnatural character of homosexuality in this way:

> *The stress falls upon the unnatural character of the vice and in that, as also in verse 27 [of Romans 1], consists the peculiar gravity of the abomination. The implication is that however grievous is fornication or adultery the desecration involved in homosexuality is on a lower plane of degeneracy; it is unnatural and therefore evinces a perversion more basic.*[81]

Obviously, none of this gives a pass to heterosexual sin; the commands to put sexual immorality and impurity to death are universal. Holiness is not just about righteous behavior but also about living in harmony with God's design for us. If God did not design us to sexually desire members of the same sex, then why would we protect that idea and rope it off from the conviction of the Word of God? "Whoever trusts in his own mind is a fool, but he who walks in wisdom will be delivered" (Proverbs 28:26).

This may sound condemning of someone who trusts Christ but also struggles with same-sex desire. It isn't intended to be. There are times when resisting sin seems nearly impossible. Every Christian knows the struggle of submitting the

---

81. John Murray, *The Epistle to the Romans* (Grand Rapids, MI: Wm. B. Eerdmans Publishing Co., 1959. One-volume reprint edition, 1982), 47.

"old man" to Christ's Lordship, but our temptations should not ultimately define us. Breaking our old habits, thought patterns, behaviors, and our own self-conception is challenging. How many times have we removed the sting of conviction by making a small concession to ourselves by saying, "That's just how I am?"

It is always easier to think of ourselves as a unique case rather than submitting our subconscious desires to the Lord. But if we want to overcome—and the scripture is clear that those who belong to Christ will overcome (Revelation 21:7–8)—then we must walk by faith and live in the reality of clear scriptural truth. "As he who called you is holy, you also be holy in all your conduct, since it is written, 'You shall be holy, for I am holy'" (1 Peter 1:15–16).

# CHAPTER 5

# CREATING
# ACTIVISTS

"Gay Christianity" has redefined scriptural passages, undermined biblical clarity, questioned historic teaching, reframed public worship, and reimagined personhood and identity. But to what end? Is there an endgame to "gay Christianity"? I believe the endgame of "gay Christianity" is to create LGBT activists and allies within the walls of the Christian church. Obviously, not every individual "gay Christian" has a stated goal of enacting a political agenda on the church. But collectively, "gay Christianity" fits perfectly within the larger political agenda of the LGBT movement to change societal attitudes and responses toward homosexuality (as an idea/condition) and homosexuals (as a social group).

In the 1989 gay rights manifesto *After the Ball: How America Will Conquer Its Fear and Hatred of Gays in the 90's*, LGBT activists Marshall Kirk and Hunter Madsen envisioned an extensive media campaign across all aspects of American culture that sought to win the public to the side of gay rights. Forgoing attempts to convince diehard opponents, the strategy was to focus on those who were ambivalent or "passively negative" toward homosexuality by making homosexuality seem normal and nonthreatening. This strategy was to be applied across every facet of society—including the Christian church. Kirk and Madsen said, "Gays can undermine the moral authority of homo-hating [conservative] churches over less fervent adherents by portraying such institutions as antiquated backwaters, badly out of step with the times and with the latest findings of psychology."[1] They argued that "with enough open talk about the prevalence and acceptability of homosexuality," the church's witness would be minimized.[2]

In many ways, this political push has not been presented as political at all. For instance, in their material geared toward churches and Christian leaders, the Human Rights Campaign (the largest LGBT lobbying group in the U.S.) keeps the political language to a minimum. And yet the stated vision of their Religion and Faith Program is this:

*The HRC Religion and Faith Program is working to create a world where nobody is forced to choose between who they are or who they love and what they believe. Thanks in part to this work, more and more faith communities aren't simply engaging in dialogue around LGBTQ equality, they're leading the conversation.*[3]

---

1. Marshall Kirk and Hunter Madsen, *After the Ball: How America Will Conquer Its Fear and Hatred of Gays in the 90's* (New York: Plume/Penguin, 1989), 179.

2. Ibid., 179.

3. Human Rights Campaign, "HRC Story," web archive snapshot March 23, 2020, https://web.archive.org/web/20200323184133/https://www.hrc.org/hrc-story/hrc-foundation.

This is a political group accomplishing a political goal through the means of local churches.

Every political cause needs an enemy; for many, the politics of conservative evangelicals are an easy target. If evangelical politics can be shown to be insensitive, unscientific, oppressive, and homophobic, then their political clout can be significantly diminished. People's personal theology matters little if they are constantly being told that they are oppressors responsible for the mistreatment of entire groups of people. And if this tactic does not win the older generations, perhaps it will work on the younger ones.

## Moving the Marriage Debate

*Our organization is not taking a theological position on the issue of the sacrament of marriage. We just want evangelicals to see that it is possible to hold a plethora of beliefs about sexuality and marriage while affirming the rights of LGBTQ men and women to be civilly married under the law.* — Brandan Robertson, spokesperson for Evangelicals for Marriage Equality[4]

In 2014, as the national debate around gay marriage intensified, a group of progressive evangelicals joined together with the stated goal of trying to change the conversation. The group called themselves Evangelicals for Marriage Equality

---

4. Religion News Service, "Progressive Evangelicals Launch Campaign to Expand Christian Support for Same-Sex Marriage," HuffPost, September 15, 2014, https://www.huffpost.com/entry/us-evangelicals-gay-marriage_n_5824174.

(EME). Their desire was to remove the intense us-versus-them tone of the marriage debate among Christians and to replace it with an in-house discussion where charitable dialogue was supposed to be central.

Even though the rhetoric behind EME focused on Christians having dialogue, there was a very particular political purpose in mind: move conservatives to be more accepting of gay marriage. And how would that happen exactly? Did conservatives need to abandon their theological arguments for traditional marriage? Not at all. They just needed to separate their politics from their theology. As EME spokesperson Brandan Robertson put it in *Time Magazine*:

> *Many evangelicals believe the Bible describes same-sex relationships as sinful; others disagree. Regardless of whether we believe that God views these relationships as sinful or not, our particular Christian definition of marriage shouldn't dictate the definition of marriage in a pluralistic and religiously diverse society such as ours.*[5]

What Robertson did was very clever. He presented the marriage debate as one marked by emotion rather than facts. But he implied that conservative theology was the emotion that needed to be removed from the debate. Likewise, he saw a pluralistic society as something that should not be unfairly hindered or challenged. He then appealed to

---

5. Brandan Robertson, "Evangelicals for Marriage Equality: The Story Behind Our Launch," *Time Magazine*, September 9, 2014, https://time.com/3308983/evangelicals-for-marriage-equality-the-story-behind-our-launch/.

religious freedom (an argument conservatives were likely to appreciate) to make it sound like conservatives were being inconsistent with their own views. He used an argument for religious freedom that would work against the religious freedom of conservative evangelicals in the long run. Though the inferences seem small, the point he was making was that politics are far more pressing than theology.

Ironically, that is an easy point for Robertson to make because his theology supports his politics. He is gay and wants to be able to marry a man one day—and he believes the Bible affirms that. Even though he makes it sound as if he is the one being charitable, he is just as strident in his position as the supposedly unreasonable conservatives. The only difference is that his secular argumentation has a lot more sway in secular society.

In June of 2015, the Supreme Court ruled on *Obergefell vs. Hodges,* which stated that the fundamental right to marry is guaranteed to same-sex couples across all states, striking down any state bans on gay marriage. Overall public support for gay marriage saw a radical reversal over the 2000s and 2010s. One study noted that support for same-sex marriage had gone from 60% opposition in 2004 to 61% approval by 2019.[6] Acceptance among evangelical Protestants grew from 11% in 2004 to 29% in 2019—a lower total than other Christian demographics, but a significant increase nevertheless.[7]

---

6. David Masci, Anna Brown, and Jocelyn Kiley, "5 Facts about Same-Sex Marriage." *Pew Research Center,* June 24, 2019, https://www.pewresearch.org/fact-tank/2019/06/24/same-sex-marriage/.

7. "Attitudes on Same-Sex Marriage," *Pew Research Center,* May 14, 2019, https://www.pewforum.org/fact-sheet/changing-attitudes-on-gay-marriage/.

Evangelicals for Marriage Equality had served its purpose and was defunct shortly after the Supreme Court decision. No one knows what the actual impact of EME was on evangelical thought overall, but the ideas they promoted have become the basic logic of many younger evangelicals. Considering that in 2020, nearly 80% of Americans under the age of 35 support same-sex marriage, it isn't surprising that many young evangelicals are joining those ranks as they become increasingly embarrassed by the cultural views of their parents.[8]

Why have Christians opposed same-sex marriage? In politics, a law or ruling might have a very specific judgment stated on the page, but it sets precedent and enshrines values. Conservatives believed the gay marriage ruling would impact religious liberty in America. Almost immediately, cases were brought against Christian business owners who did not want to violate their consciences by supporting gay weddings through their business activities. Although the Christians had constitutionally protected beliefs, their refusal to provide goods or services for gay ceremonies was seen as discrimination. One can easily envision how similar discrimination suits could be brought against conservative churches for any number of things—from marriage policies to hiring practices to public statements regarding the sinfulness of homosexuality.

Being enshrined in American law obviously does not make something permissible in God's law. But it does move

---

8. Ryan Burge, "On LGBT and Women's Equality, Stark Statistical Reality Is Coming for White Evangelicals," Religion News Service, August 7, 2020, https://religionnews.com/2020/08/07/on-lgbt-and-womens-equality-stark-statistical-reality-is-coming-for-white-evangelicals/.

the window of cultural acceptability. For instance, when sodomy laws were being heavily debated in the late 1980s, sociologists observed that "the survival of gay sodomy laws, even unenforced, sends a message to both straights and gays that homosexuality is intrinsically wrong, sinful because it's 'unnatural.'"[9] This is why gay activists focused so intently on removing those laws from the books. It was a statement of cultural values. Conversely, the legitimizing of homosexuality by redefining marriage makes the action of homosexual intercourse seem less heinous and the mindset of homosexuality more normalized. Those who desire it seem more marginalized, while those who oppose it seem crueler and more out-of-touch.

Some conservatives, like Ryan T. Anderson, argued against gay marriage from a natural law perspective (a belief that God established His creation with self-evident truths and thereby the basic social structures of our world can be understood in creation itself).

*We argue that marriage really exists to unite a man and a woman as husband and wife to then be mother and father to any children that that union creates. . . . This is based on anthropological truths that men and women are distinct and complementary. It's based on a biological fact that reproduction requires both a man and a woman. It's based on a social reality that children deserve a mom and a dad. Our argument is that this is what gets the government in the marriage*

---

9. Marshall Kirk and Hunter Madsen, *After the Ball: How America Will Conquer Its Fear and Hatred of Gays in the 90's* (New York: Plume/Penguin, 1989), 68.

*business. It's not because the state cares about consenting adult romance.*[10]

Still, the Christian argument against gay marriage will always be grounded in a theological conviction regarding homosexuality because our politics are shaped by those fundamental beliefs. The Christian worldview recognizes that to live according to God's design is actually good for people individually (Proverbs 1:8–9) and good for society as a whole (Deuteronomy 5:33) because goodness is not determined by people's feelings but by God Himself (Psalm 34:14). The Christian worldview also recognizes that unbelieving mankind will oppose God (Romans 8:7) and that laws and governments are one of the ways in which God's rule is resisted (Psalm 2:1–3). When something evil becomes seen as good, society suffers and God's wrath is kindled (Romans 1:18), waiting to be fully unleashed until the measure of sin has been filled (1 Thessalonians 2:14–16). For the good of society, the clarity of the truth, the safety of the church and the love of our neighbors (yes, even our LGBT neighbors), faithful Christians have opposed and continue to oppose same-sex marriage.

---

10. Robert Barnes, "The Right Finds a Fresh Voice on Same-Sex Marriage," *The Washington Post,* April 15, 2015, https://www.washingtonpost.com/politics/courts_law/a-fresh-face-emerges-as-a-leader-in-the-movement-against-same-sex-marriage/2015/04/15/d78cf256-dece-11e4-be40-566e2653afe5_story.html.

## Blaming Evangelicals

*Reminder that LGBTQ kids who are not affirmed by their families are more likely to attempt suicide. And it just takes one attempt for us to lose them. Don't risk that. Give your child the best chance at life. Love them and let them flourish.* — Kevin Garcia, gay theologian and author[11]

Few appeals carry more emotional weight than the thought of being personally responsible for another person's death—especially the death of a child. Activists recognize this and have utilized the high suicide rate of LGBT youth to their advantage. It is widely recognized that people identifying as LGBT are more likely to attempt suicide than those who identify as straight; some say as much as five times more likely.[12] One report noted that in 2017, 5.9% of U.S. adolescents who identified as heterosexual attempted suicide, while 20.1% of adolescents who identified as lesbian, gay, bisexual, or "not sure" attempted suicide that year.[13] The Anxiety and Depression Association of America claims that LGBT people are up to 2.5 times more likely to deal with anxiety and

11. Kevin Garcia (@theKevinGarcia), "Reminder that LGBTQ kids who are not affirmed by their families are more likely to attempt suicide. And it just takes one attempt for us to lose them…" Twitter, February 27, 2020, 7:06 AM, https://twitter.com/theKevinGarcia_/status/1233015497295384576.

12. "Preventing Suicide: Facts about Suicide." *The Trevor Project,* accessed August 9, 2021, https://www.thetrevorproject.org/resources/preventing-suicide/facts-about-suicide/

13. Julia Raifman et al, "Sexual Orientation and Suicide Attempt Disparities among US Adolescents: 2007–2017," *Pediatrics: Official Journal of the American Academy of Pediatrics* 145, no. 3 (March 2020): e20191658, https://doi.org/10.1542/peds.2019-1658.

depression in their lives than straight and nontrans people.[14]

The implication embedded in the typical citation of these statistics is that LGBT people would have depression and suicide rates more comparable to heterosexuals if they were in more affirming societies. This is a theory called *minority stress theory*—the idea that stigmatized minority groups face higher levels of stress than those of majority, nonstigmatized groups, which leads to poorer health outcomes over time. "We don't just need an individual approach to reduce [LGBT youth] stress," says Ryan J. Watson, assistant professor of human development at the University of Connecticut. "We need a societal approach, and we hope our research findings will help inform policy and practice changes to improve the lives of these young people."[15]

The problem with these statistics will always be a question of interpretation. One of the most noted maxims of statistical research is "correlation does not imply causation," yet this whole theory of LGBT suicidality hinges upon it. Meanwhile, there are counterexamples that show that even with increased legal changes and social acceptance, LGBT people are still at increased risk of suicide. For instance, Denmark and Sweden have been noted for some of the most progressive LGBT policies in the world. Denmark was the first country to recognize civil unions for same-sex couples in 1989, while

---

14. Brad Brenner, "Understanding Anxiety and Depression for LGBT People," Anxiety and Depression Association of America (ADAA), updated October 2020, https://adaa.org/learn-from-us/from-the-experts/blog-posts/consumer/understanding-anxiety-and-depression-lgbtq.

15. Maureen Connolly and Margot Slade, "The United States of Stress 2019," Everyday Health, May 7, 2019, https://www.everydayhealth.com/wellness/united-states-of-stress/.

Sweden followed suit in 1995. Denmark officially legalized gay marriage in June 2012, while Sweden did so in May 2009. Nevertheless, a study of data from these two nations spanning 1989 to 2016 found some unexpected results:

*In this study, the largest of its kind to date, more than 28,500 individuals who entered a same-sex marriage were followed for an average of over 11 years. Overall, this group was found to be 2.3 times more likely to die by suicide compared to individuals who entered an opposite-sex marriage during the same period.*[16]

One of the lead authors of the study added:

*Our findings suggest that persons in same-sex marriages may be experiencing declining levels of stigma, although it is troubling that our study confirms an excess of suicide deaths in same-sex-married persons. One could consider our findings from Denmark and Sweden, which are among the leading countries in same-sex rights, as the "best case"-scenario.*[17]

This is not the only such example from nations with progressive LGBT policies and broad social acceptance. A study from the Netherlands in 2006 summarized their findings on male suicidality and sexual orientation: "This

16. Gunnar Andersson and Ann Haas, "Excess Suicide Rate among Same-Sex Married Is Decreasing in the Nordic Countries," Stockholm University: Demography Unit, Department of Sociology, November 15, 2019, https://www.suda.su.se/about-us/press-media-news/excess-suicide-rate-among-same-sex-married-is-decreasing-in-the-nordic-countries-1.462698.

17. Ibid.

study suggests that even in a country with a comparatively tolerant climate regarding homosexuality, homosexual men were at much higher risk for suicidality than heterosexual men."[18] A 2017 study on adolescent suicide from Canada admitted, "We see decreases in suicidal behaviour for heterosexual adolescents, but not in the same way for many sexual minority youth, despite advances in social acceptance of gay, lesbian, and bisexual issues in North America."[19] Even though definitive causes cannot be discerned and these studies admit their findings plainly, the general consensus continues to be that these are examples of society's failure to be fully affirming. We simply must work harder, they say.

With the seemingly unassailable assertion that social stigma and homophobia are behind LGBT mental anguish, it does not take long before Christianity is wrapped up in that assertion as well. "Conservative religions in the US often push WRONG beliefs that stigmatize LGBTQ people and that take a huge and unnecessary human toll," says activist James Finn. "Accepting doctrines that ignore human knowledge while scapegoating innocent people isn't good, isn't moral, isn't acceptable."[20] Shannon T.L. Kearns, the first openly transgender man ordained to the Old Catholic priesthood,

---

18. Ron de Graaf, Theo G.M. Sandfort, and Margreet ten Have, "Suicidality and Sexual Orientation: Differences between Men and Women in a General Population-Based Sample from the Netherlands," *Archives of Sexual Behavior* 35, no. 3 (June 2006): 253–262, https://doi.org/10.1007/s10508-006-9020-z.

19. Tracey Peter et al, "Trends in Suicidality among Sexual Minority and Heterosexual Students in a Canadian Population-Based Cohort Study," *Psychology of Sexual Orientation and Gender Diversity* 4, no. 1 (March 2017): 115–123, https://doi.org/10.1037/sgd0000211.

20. James Finn, "The Third Rail of LGBTQ Activism," Medium, August 23, 2019, https://medium.com/james-finn/the-third-rail-of-lgbtq-activism-3fa9368bce4b.

declares, "I think evangelical theology is toxic from stem to stern. There is nothing in it that is redeemable and it kills the people it touches. . . . Evangelicalism is abuse. It's toxic, not just to queer people but to all people."[21]

These assertions are gaining momentum—especially now that a handful of recent studies on LGBT religiosity and suicidality are making the rounds on outlets like the HuffPost.[22] For instance, a 2018 survey of college-enrolled young adults aged 18–24 found:

*Increased importance of religion was associated with higher odds of recent suicide ideation for both gay/lesbian and questioning students. . . . Lesbian/gay students who viewed religion as very important had greater odds for recent suicidal ideation and lifetime suicide attempt compared with heterosexual individuals.[23]*

The study concluded, "Religion-based services for mental health and suicide prevention may not benefit gay/lesbian, bisexual, or questioning individuals."[24]

A 2020 study from the same group of researchers found that heterosexuals participating in Christian/Catholic denominations had 24–37% reduced odds of suicidal ideation

21. Shannon T. L. Kearns, "When We Call Abuse Love," Queer Theology, accessed August 9, 2021, https://www.queertheology.com/when-we-call-abuse-love/.

22. Carol Kuruvilla, "Chilling Study Sums Up Link between Religion and Suicide for Queer Youth," HuffPost, April 18, 2018 (updated April 19, 2018), https://www.huffpost.com/entry/queer-youth-religion-suicide-study_n_5ad4f7b3e4b077c89ceb9774

23. Megan C. Lytle et al, "Association of Religiosity with Sexual Minority Suicide Ideation and Attempt," *American Journal of Preventative Medicine* 54, no. 5 (May 2018): 644–651, https://doi.org/10.1016/j.amepre.2018.01.019.

24. Ibid.

relative to heterosexual atheists/agnostics. However, the study also found that for lesbian, gay, and bisexually identified people, participants in those Christian denominations had 68–77% increased odds of suicidal ideation relative to atheist/agnostic LGB people. To put an even finer point on it, the study declared, "Unspecified Christian and Catholic sexual minorities had 184% and 198% increased odds of recent suicidal ideation compared to Unitarian/Universalist sexual minorities."[25]

In response to these studies, it should be noted that suicidal ideation can include anything from actively seeking to kill oneself to sometimes passively wishing not to live. The range is wide and far more subjective than documenting suicide attempts or deaths by suicide. For instance, the numbers for the suicide rate are collated from deaths by suicide rather than suicidal ideation. This doesn't make the ideation any less tragic, but it is recognized as a more objective measurement.

Furthermore, while it may sound insensitive to say so, we must also recognize the reality that suicide is an act of the will. It might come out of a sense of helplessness, deep desperation, and mental anguish—and it may be exacerbated by conflicts with other people—but it is still a choice that can be avoided. Tragically, suicide always leaves behind hurt and confused loved ones who are often unsure as to the actual reasons. But as society moves away from the concept of personal responsibility toward views of systemic injustice, even an individual's choice to end their own life will be seen

---

25. John R. Blosnich et al, "Questions of Faith: Religious Affiliations and Suicidal Ideation among Sexual Minority Young Adults," *Suicide & Life-Threatening Behavior,* August 2020, https://doi.org/10.1111/sltb.12679.

more and more as someone else's fault.

Still, Christians are met with a challenge: What about the LGBT-identified people who believe the conservative church is in some way responsible for their suicidal thoughts? Christians want to alleviate people's suffering and help them live whole and happy lives. But Christians also know that joy and contentedness are found by having a relationship with God and living in harmony with His plan for us. Adjusting our teaching, language, or approach to homosexuality in order to affirm people in their desires will not honor the Lord or automatically ease people's burdens.

Imagine all the conflicting information being presented in our culture today. This book has covered a large assortment of it: confusion about scripture's teaching, about correct theology, about sin, about psychology, about sexual identity, about political policy, about what happiness is, about the nature of reality itself. Voices on one side say gay is OK; voices on another say it is an abomination. Voices on one side say that Christianity should be rejected or altered; voices on another say that Christ is the only way to have peace with God.

Add in the traumatic experiences of a person's life and real pains they have felt. Add in a feeling of being attracted to the same sex and some desire to identify as a Christian. Add in the reality of spiritual warfare and demonic oppression. Altogether, these are not small burdens, and it is not my purpose to minimize them. But they will not suddenly vanish if societies, families, or churches become more affirming.

Furthermore, because God's law is true and homosexual desire is unnatural, it's not surprising that a burden of guilt goes along with it. This is a mercy of God, and it is not our job to weaken the weight of conviction with the cheap substitute of affirmation. God's grace is sufficient for every sinner, yet the way our burden of sin is removed is to confess it to the Lord and seek His forgiveness. We cannot and should not offer peace where only Christ can.

Christian ministry is not a ministry of people-pleasing (Galatians 1:10). Christians want others to know the peace of Christ—as a matter of justification before God (Romans 5:1) as well as experientially in their real-life feelings (2 Thessalonians 3:16). But the peace of Christ is available only to those who are surrendered to Christ by faith (Isaiah 26:3). There might be feelings of discomfort and pain as people hear a message of hope and healing—for the Enemy would love nothing more than to pluck away the seeds of the gospel sown in the heart (Matthew 13:19), to bring tribulation of life and mind to the one who might receive it eagerly (Matthew 13:20–21), and to bring to mind the cares of the world that choke out the Word over time (Matthew 13:22). God's grace is freely given (it isn't earned by our efforts), yet we know that following Christ is costly, and it is a cost too high for some (Luke 14:25–33). But the message of Christ will not be a hard burden for the person who truly wants to take on the yoke of Christ by humble faith (Matthew 11:28–30).

If Romans 1 is true and homosexuality is one form of suppressing the truth in unrighteousness, then it is no surprise that LGBT people are at elevated risk of mental health issues overall. When the spiritual implications of homosexuality are taught clearly, we would expect to find people resisting, suppressing, and arguing against the truth.

But the answer is not to jettison scriptural truth or soften the actual cost of discipleship by helping someone "reconcile their faith with their sexuality."

However, where the truth is clearly expounded, we would also expect to see saints of God being established, equipped, and growing in grace. Christ offers the only answer to the turmoil of soul that many LGBT people are suffering, and it is a different answer from what the world offers (John 14:27). If we lose that, then there will be no hope for anyone—for all have sinned and fall short of God's glory (Romans 3:23), everyone is called to die to themselves (Mark 8:35), and everyone who follows Christ must take up a cross (Matthew 10:38).

## Banning Conversion Therapy

*Conversion therapy reinforces internalized homophobia, anxiety, guilt and depression. It leads to self-loathing and emotional and psychological harm when change doesn't happen. Regrettably, too many will choose suicide as a result of their sense of failure.* — Open letter from former "ex-gay" ministry leaders now opposing conversion therapy [26]

*Conversion therapy* is a complicated subject, if only because activists have filled the term with any number of meanings. It has also become a polarized political issue, with many

---

26. Tony Merevick, "Exclusive: 9 Former Ex-Gay Leaders Join Movement to Ban Conversion Therapy," BuzzFeed, July 31, 2014, https://www.buzzfeed.com/tonymerevick/exclusive-9-former-ex-gay-leaders-join-movement-to-ban-gay-c.

states issuing bans on the practice. This leads many people to feel it is unsafe and harmful, even though few can actually define it. The term itself has become a taboo label that some activists have lobbed generally on anyone who believes that a person's sexual orientation can be changed. This labeling poses a threat to the Christian worldview as well as how we think about Christian conversion and sanctification.

There are many layers of confusion and misinformation about conversion therapy that must be worked through in order to understand the debate. They break down into roughly six questions:

1. What exactly does *conversion therapy* mean?

2. Does conversion therapy use electroshock treatment?

3. Is conversion therapy just a "pray away the gay" idea?

4. Is conversion therapy effective?

5. Is conversion therapy harmful?

6. How should Christians think about conversion therapy?

The first layer is the ambiguity and looseness of the term *conversion therapy*. Generally, *conversion therapy* (sometimes called *reparative therapy*) is a broad term for any group or person trying to change another person's sexual orientation. A more precise term (though a more verbose one) is *sexual orientation change effort* (SOCE). When critics of SOCE use the phrase *conversion therapy*, they usually leave several questions unaddressed and undefined: (1) Who is practicing it? (2) What are they doing? (3) Why are they doing it? and (4) What impact is it having? The term can imply anything from physical torture to naive prayer groups to outright brainwashing. This ambiguity is intentional and is very effective in creating a conversion therapy bogeyman and straw man in the public eye.

The second layer is the false idea that conversion therapy uses painful methods like electroshock therapy to cure homosexuality. In the 1960s and 70s—when homosexuality was still classified as a mental illness—there were some secular psychiatrists who tested the use of electroshock aversion therapy in the treatment of homosexuality.[27] *Aversion therapy* combines an unwanted behavior with a negative effect designed to make the patient give up the unwanted behavior by associating it with discomfort. Aversion therapy has been used to help patients break addictions to alcohol, drugs, cigarettes, gambling, and even anger management issues.[28] Psychiatrists debate the effectiveness of aversion therapy in general and now dismiss it entirely when it relates to homosexuality—seeing the use of electroshock as the physical abuse that it was. Although the terms sound phonetically similar, *aversion therapy* and *conversion therapy* are two different concepts, though they have often been erroneously linked together in the debate.

The third layer is the idea that conversion therapy is an effort to get people to "pray away the gay." This is what activists claim is happening with what have been labelled

---

27. M. J. MacCulloch and M.P. Feldman, "Aversion Therapy in the Management of 43 Homosexuals," *British Medical Journal,* June 3, 1967, 594–597, https://www.ncbi.nlm. nih.gov/pmc/articles/PMC1842087/.

28. Kendra Cherry, "Aversion Therapy Uses and Effectiveness," verywellmind, March 26, 2020, https://www.verywellmind.com/what-is-aversion-therapy-2796001.

"ex-gay" ministries. These are Christian counseling ministries to people with unwanted same-sex attraction—frequently led by men and women who have come out of a gay or lesbian lifestyle. The ministries usually have a spiritual focus—emphasizing prayer, biblical counseling, Bible study, and group accountability.

"Ex-gay" ministries have undergone intense scrutiny in recent years, especially in light of some former "ex-gay" leaders closing their ministries and changing their position on the possibility of orientation change. These stories play prominently in media coverage of the conversion therapy debate. There is certainly room to critique anyone who has given the false impression that the Christian life is a simple formula whereby sin is overcome forever. But the idea that people would instantly overcome their sinful temptations was more often a mischaracterization by critics of Christianity or the impression of struggling people who wanted an easy solution to their trouble.

Biblically faithful "ex-gay" ministries emphasize the gospel's power to transform—pointing to the need to repent of sin and be born again. This emphasis on *personal spiritual conversion* (repenting from sin and trusting Christ) is easy to misrepresent as an immediate cure to sin's influence in a person's life because having the Holy Spirit indwelling a believer enables sanctification. Likewise, prayer is an essential part of personal discipleship and Christian maturity, yet it is not an instantaneous cure-all for temptation and wrong desire. Unsurprisingly, these spiritual priorities are mocked and dismissed by the world.

The fourth layer is the idea that conversion therapy is

completely ineffective. The definition of change that activists hold up is frequently the idea of a "flipped switch"—100% eradication of every desire, inclination, temptation, and thought toward homosexuality. Instantaneous healing is not something that counselors or therapists dealing with any condition would guarantee to people. As Peter Sprigg notes in his research on SOCE:

> *If a client experiences any significant reduction in homosexual attractions or behaviors, or increase in heterosexual attractions, as a result of SOCE, then that process can be considered "effective," and many clients would consider it a success, even if some or occasional same-sex attractions remain.*[29]

Many studies have found that sexual orientation change is possible. One of the most interesting was released in 2003 by secular psychiatrist Robert L. Spitzer, who had played a major role in the American Psychiatric Association's move to no longer treat homosexuality as a mental disorder. Spitzer interviewed 200 individuals (143 males, 57 females) and concluded:

> *Some gay men and lesbians, following reparative therapy, report that they have made major changes from a predominantly homosexual orientation to a predominantly heterosexual orientation. The changes following reparative therapy were not limited to sexual behavior and sexual orientation*

29. Peter Sprigg, "Are Sexual Orientation Change Efforts (SOCE) Effective? Are They Harmful? What the Evidence Shows," Family Research Council, Issue Analysis IS18101, September 2018, https://www.frc.org/issueanalysis/are-sexual-orientation-change-efforts-soce-effective-are-they-harmful-what-the-evidence-shows.

*self-identity. The changes encompassed sexual attraction, arousal, fantasy, yearning, and being bothered by homosexual feelings. The changes encompassed the core aspects of sexual orientation.*[30]

Though most therapists would not claim universal results, many have cited legitimate results of lasting change.

The fifth layer is the idea that conversion therapy is harmful to LGBT people. This is the public perception, reinforced by activists such as Sam Brinton or Brielle Goldani, who report that they were shipped off to conversion therapy camps when they were young where they were physically and psychologically tortured. While they are able to provide extensive detail as to the horrific treatment they supposedly received at these camps, they are not able to give verifiable information about where exactly these treatment centers were located, what year these events happened, or the names of the people and organizations involved.[31] This is not uncommon, as many of the supposed horror stories of conversion therapy abuse are anecdotal and do not provide enough details to be verified.

Many activists recognize how unreliable the extreme cases are, so they simply argue that the expectation of change puts undue stress on gay people and makes them more depressive and suicidal. This is a claim that the studies of SOCE effectiveness have also debunked. One survey of 125 religious

---

30. Robert L. Spitzer, "Can Some Gay Men and Lesbians Change Their Sexual Orientation? 200 Participants Reporting a Change from Homosexual to Heterosexual Orientation," *Archives of Sexual Behavior* 32, no. 5 (2003): 413.

31. Peter Sprigg, "Truth Matters in the Ex-Gay Debate," *LifeSite News*, September 2, 2014, https://www.lifesitenews.com/opinion/truth-matters-in-ex-gay-debate.

men who sought out orientation therapy concluded, "On the basis of this survey, religious clients could be told that some degree of change is likely from SOCE, and positive change in suicidality, self-esteem, depression, self-harm, substance abuse, social functioning should be moderate to marked [improvement]."[32]

Their figures were overall consistent with the effectiveness and perceived harm of other therapy treatments. Even the APA has not been consistent in stating the harmfulness of SOCE. In 1998, the group took a more neutral stance, believing there was a lack of scientific evidence proving it was harmful.[33] Then, in 2013—citing no new evidence—they called on lawmakers to "ban the harmful and discriminatory practice."[34]

The sixth layer is the Christian response. It seems obvious that a conflict of ideologies is at work in the debate over conversion therapy. Is homosexuality innate and immutable? Did God make people homosexual? If not—and there is no scriptural basis to say that He has—then the existence of homosexuality in mankind is a result of living in a fallen world (Romans 3:23) and all people being marred by sin (Psalm 51:5).

---

32. Paul L. Santero, Neil E. Whitehead, and Dolores Ballesteros, "Effects of Therapy on Religious Men Who Have Unwanted Same-Sex Attraction," *The Linacre Quarterly,* July 23, 2018, https://journals.sagepub.com/doi/abs/10.1177/0024363918788559.

33. "Therapies Focused on Attempts to Change Sexual Orientation (Reparative or Conversion Therapies) Position Statement," American Psychiatric Association, December 1998, https://web.archive.org/web/20110407082738/http://www.psych.org/Departments/EDU/Library/APAOfficialDocumentsandRelated/PositionStatements/200001.aspx.

34. "APA Reiterates Strong Opposition to Conversion Therapy," American Psychiatric Association, November 15, 2018, https://www.psychiatry.org/newsroom/news-releases/apa-reiterates-strong-opposition-to-conversion-therapy.

The narrative that critics of conversion therapy want to promote is that homosexuality is normal, good, and should be celebrated. As the activist group Born Perfect says, their mission is "to end conversion therapy and ensure that every child knows that they are born perfect."[35] Activist John Smid says that the problem with conversion therapy is the message that gay people are "broken and sick and they need to be repaired."[36] This presents a direct assault on biblical language and biblical thinking. We are being told that people are ultimately defined by their sexual orientation and must be free to live out that orientation in whatever way makes them happiest. Any attempt to speak differently is said to lead LGBT people to anxiety, shame, and potential suicide.

The Bible says we are not "born perfect." Rather, we are unclean, condemned sinners with nothing good to commend us to God (Isaiah 64:6). But this doesn't mean we are without hope: "God shows his love for us in that while we were still sinners, Christ died for us" (Romans 5:8). The gospel of Jesus Christ is the only hope any human has for peace with God and power to overcome the sin that so easily ensnares us. This should be front and center in any attempt to deal with persistent sin patterns and defiling passions. The Bible further tells us that Christians are no longer ruled by the flesh and therefore can live free from slavery to fleshly lusts (Romans 8:12–14), which means that transforming change is possible (1 Corinthians 6:11). If that is true, then Christians should

35. Born Perfect, accessed August 6, 2021, https://bornperfect.org.

36. Tony Merevick, "Exclusive: 9 Former Ex-Gay Leaders Join Movement to Ban Conversion Therapy," BuzzFeed, July 31, 2014, https://www.buzzfeed.com/tonymerevick/exclusive-9-former-ex-gay-leaders-join-movement-to-ban-gay-c.

look skeptically at the assertion that people are born gay and cannot change.

When it comes to conversion therapy, sadly, not all counselors are biblical and not all people seeking to overcome their sin are truly willing to humble themselves before God. Both elements can and have coincided in the history of conversion therapy. Counselors should be examined on their individual merits and carefully considered before being sought out. The cases of physical abuse appear overblown, but if physical abuses are truly taking place somewhere, then the culprits should be examined, exposed, and prosecuted accordingly. However, Christians should be aware of how the conversion therapy debate is being framed and manipulated. The push is not just to shutter conversion therapy groups but to completely eradicate the view that there is something inherently wrong in being a homosexual.

There are many faithful "ex-gay" ministries seeking to help men and women find freedom from their bondage to sexual sin—and having success doing so. They now find themselves in the crosshairs of LGBT activists who would love nothing more than to see these ministries shuttered and the ministers imprisoned. But underneath the attacks on "ex-gay" ministries is a question about the power of the gospel itself: If the church only has a gospel without power to transform, then what does it truly have?

# What's the Problem?

*Woe to those who call evil good and good evil, who put darkness for light and light for darkness, who put bitter for sweet and sweet for bitter!* — Isaiah 5:20

The ideas, attitudes, and expressions of "gay Christianity" will always work toward a political end because it desires to establish and normalize homosexuality. It cannot legitimately do it through the church, so it must attempt to do it through the state. It says that same-sex marriage must be affirmed—not only as legally permissible but as a civic good to be honored and cherished. It says that calling homosexuality a sin is the true sin—responsible for anxiety, depression, and even suicide. It says that expecting a transformation in a Christian's behavior and desires is unfair and un-Christlike—laying heavy burdens on others.

With all of those statements ringing in the ears of well-meaning Christians, what is the intended result? Change. Change of theology. Change of politics. Change of posture. Change of tone. Change of emphasis. As much as we might wish that politics are beside the point, politics are precisely the point. And politics have spiritual implications.

This is where Christians are feeling the pressure. Politics are the arena where the clash of worldviews between Christianity and secularism is most clearly felt. And many Christians are being worn down and won over in the fight. As future generations grow up immersed in a culture of LGBT acceptance, inclusion, gender confusion, and sexual autonomy, they will look at the values of previous generations of Christians as backwards, outdated, and bigoted. Indeed, it is already happening.

One LGBT activist on *HuffPost* explains:

> *In the final analysis, it's really simple. The homosexual agenda, indeed the LGBTQ agenda, is the human agenda: life, liberty and the pursuit of happiness. If you oppose that, then you are a bigot, even if you believe that the creator of the universe agrees with you.*[37]

This is LGBT activism at its heart: loathing Christians for their biblical convictions and shouting them into silent submission politically. In an ironic twist, this push against Christianity is thought of by many as justice.

However, biblical justice is not simply perceived fairness or equity, as many people in our day like to define it. Justice is God's righteousness applied to all people and all situations without partiality (Deuteronomy 1:17). When we talk about the justice of God, we are talking about justice that is rooted in the truth of God, in line with His character as reflected in His law (Exodus 20:1–2). The law includes duties to God and duties to others (Matthew 22:36–40), and both aspects are inseparably tied together (Galatians 5:14). This is fundamental to any discussion of what it means for Christians to act justly or love our neighbor.

At the end of Romans 1, Paul describes humanity's blatant refusal to acknowledge God or to live by God's law.

---

37. Joe Wenke, "The Human Agenda." HuffPost, October 12, 2013 (updated February 2, 2016), https://www.huffpost.com/entry/the-human-agenda_b_4071375.

In their refusal, God gives them over to a debased mind. A long list of sins and sinful patterns is provided in verses 29–31, covering both outwardly wicked sins against others and secret sins of the heart. Then, in Romans 1:32, Paul gives a striking statement of just how deep the sin goes: "Though they know God's righteous decree that those who practice such things deserve to die, they not only do them but give approval to those who practice them."

It isn't just that individuals want to embrace sin for themselves. It is that they also want to be approved by others and give approval to others who practice sin. Society is being built in defiance of God; community is being shaped in defiance of God. This is the way of the world, and it is the endgame of "gay Christianity."

# THE CALL TO FAITHFULNESS

*Keep a close watch on yourself and on the teaching. Persist in
this, for by so doing you will save both yourself and your hearers.*
— 1 Timothy 4:16

Does any of this really matter? As you began reading
this book, maybe that question was in your mind. Is "gay
Christianity" really that big a deal? Is it really necessary for
Christians to be unified in our understanding of homosexuality? Should this be an issue that separates faithful churches
from unfaithful churches? If we're all sinners, why make such
a big deal about this particular sin? These are the kinds of
questions posed by those who defend homosexuality within
the Christian church. But the case, at this point, should be
clear. Yes, these things matter deeply because they are matters
of faithfulness to God and to His Word.

The church of Jesus Christ is called to be a faithful
witness in both her doctrine and her life. The apostle Paul
charged Timothy to keep a close watch on both—for
Timothy's own sake as well as the souls of his hearers. In
fact, failure to be diligent in this task has already led some to
spiritual ruin (1 Timothy 1:19). While our obedience does

not earn us God's favor (Ephesians 2:8–9), God has created us to walk in obedience to His will (Ephesians 2:10). When our witness is clear, others have cause to give glory to God (Matthew 5:14–16). Even when people reject us, Christ is still being honored by our lives, and God's work is still being done through our witness (2 Corinthians 2:14–16).

What does an unfaithful witness look like? There are numerous warnings across the New Testament epistles to be on guard against those who would lead the church astray:

> *But false prophets also arose among the people, just as there will be false teachers among you, who will secretly bring in destructive heresies, even denying the Master who bought them, bringing upon themselves swift destruction. And many will follow their sensuality, and because of them the way of truth will be blasphemed.* (2 Peter 2:1–2)

What do modern-day Christians imagine a "destructive heresy" to sound like? Does it sound like loud boasts? Does it sound like folly? Does it sound like sensuality? Does it sound like someone promising freedom who is unable to break free of their own corruption?

In 2 Peter 2, it is interesting how quickly Peter links false teaching with sensuality. False teachers always appeal to our senses, to our emotions, and to our base instincts. They minimize scripture, reframe it, change the emphasis, and twist it until it is forced to confess a lie.

> *For, speaking loud boasts of folly, they entice by sensual passions of the flesh those who are barely escaping from those who live*

*in error. They promise them freedom, but they themselves are*
*slaves of corruption. For whatever overcomes a person, to that*
*he is enslaved.* (2 Peter 2:18–19)

They boast with their lies, they lead people astray, and their
judgment will be severe: "For them the gloom of utter
darkness has been reserved" (2 Peter 2:18).

Many Christians shy away from thinking through the
issue of "gay Christianity" because it doesn't seem that
pressing. It seems secondary; it seems to hurt our witness in
the world; it seems to make people our enemies who don't
have to be. It's too incendiary, too negative, too divisive. We
can craft lengthy, nuanced positions on why the issues are
more complicated than they used to be or why, for the sake
of our mission of loving sinners, we need to be more delicate
and empathetic. We can check our posture and our tone, di-
minishing the severity of scripture through our winsomeness.

The scriptural truth about homosexuality is not nearly so
complicated as we have made it seem over the past 50 years.
God made us male and female. Homosexuality is an abomination. Those who practice it have no part in the kingdom
of God. Those who desire it are dishonored and degraded by
their passions. Such were some of you. God rescues sinners
from their bondage to sin and transforms them by His grace.

These are unembellished scriptural statements. Yet there
are hundreds of evangelical pastors across this country—
some who call themselves conservatives—who would wince
at these statements, ready to add their caveats and equivoca-
tions. Perhaps we simply love our comfort. Perhaps we want
the world's praise. Perhaps we have our own hidden sins.

Perhaps we know not the scriptures or the power of God.

We find an illustration and warning about hidden sin in the book of Joshua. After God had commanded the people of Israel not to take any of the things devoted to destruction when they conquered Jericho (Joshua 6:18–19), a man named Achan disobeyed God's command, and the Lord held it against the entire nation (Joshua 7:1). This unfaithfulness led to failure in their next campaign at Ai (Joshua 7:4–5). When Joshua saw the defeat, he tore his clothes and fell down on his face before the Lord (Joshua 7:6). Joshua's heartfelt prayer was true but sounds despairing, attempting to rouse God to action on behalf of His trembling people (Joshua 7:7–9). Perhaps Joshua thought of himself as a bit like Abraham, needing God's reassurance that He truly was for them (Genesis 15:1–5).

Instead, God's response was abrupt and shockingly forthright:

> *The Lord said to Joshua, "Get up! Why have you fallen on your face? Israel has sinned; they have transgressed my covenant that I commanded them; they have taken some of the devoted things; they have stolen and lied and put them among their own belongings."* (Joshua 7:10–11)

Indeed, Joshua had to deal with the sin in the midst of the camp before they could proceed because God's hand was now against them (Joshua 7:25–26).

Does God's anger burn likewise against the unfaithfulness of many of His own churches in America? As we toy with the fringes of sin, tweaking our unfaithfulness to make it sound agreeable and holy, many ministers likely fall down and moan to God about the ineffectiveness of their ministries. Meanwhile, sin is hidden in the midst of the people— adultery, abortion, slander, embezzlement, drunkenness, homosexuality, hating, lying, sexual immorality, and whatever else is contrary to sound doctrine. It may be passively tolerated or even boldly affirmed. The Lord opposes it. And He may oppose us until we repent (Revelation 2:5).

Can the Christian faith and the LGBT movement really live in harmony? We all know the answer to that question: "For what partnership has righteousness with lawlessness? Or what fellowship has light with darkness?" (2 Corinthians 6:14). To embrace homosexuality is to embrace lawlessness, and to embrace lawlessness is to defy God. There cannot be harmony because the Christian faith is fundamentally against the rise and spread of lawlessness. The "gay Christian" movement may make it sound nice and agreeable, but it is an attack on the purity and faithfulness of Christ's church. One day it will be judged by Christ for the lies it spread in His name and the people it led astray.

The Christian faith can stand in opposition to wicked cultural movements while also preaching the gospel to sinners. In fact, it must do both. Whether sinners come to us wounded or defiant, God's amazing grace can soften the most hardened among us and heal our deepest wounds. "Believe in the Lord Jesus Christ, and you shall be saved!" (Acts 16:31).

*Since then we have a great high priest who has passed through the heavens, Jesus, the Son of God, let us hold fast our*

211

*confession. For we do not have a high priest who is unable to sympathize with our weaknesses, but one who in every respect has been tempted as we are, yet without sin. Let us then with confidence draw near to the throne of grace, that we may receive mercy and find grace to help in time of need.* (Hebrews 4:14–16)

Even though the forces of darkness are opposed to the life and teaching of the church, Christ Himself has declared that "the gates of hell shall not prevail against it" (Matthew 16:18). We are His ambassadors and are not free to change the message to make it more palatable. While Christ has promised that His church will prevail, He has not promised that all who call themselves Christians will persevere until the end.

*And then many will fall away and betray one another and hate one another. And many false prophets will arise and lead many astray. And because lawlessness will be increased, the love of many will grow cold. But the one who endures to the end will be saved.* (Matthew 24:10–13)

Many will shift; many will compromise; many will fall away; many will give up in the fight. Only those who are truly united to Christ will endure to the end.

All the more reason to "guard the good deposit entrusted to you" (2 Timothy 1:14) and to "share in suffering as a good soldier of Christ Jesus" (2 Timothy 2:3). The world can mock us. It can call us homophobes and bigots and haters and anything else. But if we love Christ and love others, then we have no reason to fear because our reward is in heaven. We live before His face and submit ourselves to His will.

The teaching of "gay Christianity" is false and must be exposed for what it is—a "destructive heresy," to use Peter's words. It is dangerous to affirm what God calls an abomination, shameful, and dishonorable. It is unloving to make people feel at ease in their sinful desires and behavior. It is un-Christlike to call evil "good" and good "evil." And all of these things dishonor our Lord, who "who gave himself for us to redeem us from all lawlessness and to purify for himself a people for his own possession who are zealous for good works" (Titus 2:14). So let that be our guiding principle as we step out by faith into a world that hates us to share the truth of Almighty God who came to rescue sinners by the blood of His Son.

*But we are not of those who shrink back and are destroyed, but of those who have faith and preserve their souls.* — Hebrews 10:39

# ACKNOWLEDGMENTS

I did not set out initially to write a book about "gay Christianity." Rather, I began simply by trying to help my fellow American Family Studios producers research topics for our documentary *In His Image: Delighting in God's Plan for Gender and Sexuality*. My specific task in that process was to understand the emergence of "gay Christianity" within the church. Where did it come from? What were the arguments for it? Where was the movement heading? What I discovered in that research eventually became the book that you hold in your hands.

Books are always the result of the input and shaping of many unseen influences. I am grateful for the leadership of American Family Association that saw value in my research and wanted me to expand it into book form. Senior Vice President Buddy Smith and Executive Vice President Ed Vitagliano, in particular, gave valuable feedback in the early stages. They have helped me understand how to take a complicated topic and craft something clear and beneficial for the AFA audience. But even more, they encouraged me to remain focused on God's Word, allowing that to guide my critique of pro-gay arguments more than anything else.

My immediate coworkers in American Family Studios helped me maintain stamina throughout the rigorous process of writing and drafting revisions. Austin Brooks, Kendra White, Kyle Benson, Maize Warren, and Jon Yerby are people I am blessed to work alongside and consider close friends. As filmmakers, we often work in collaboration. This project was different in that it consisted primarily of me working alone, but the mutual edification and strengthening of good conversations proved just as essential for this book as it has for any of our film projects.

Other AFA coworkers who directly helped me shape this work are Wil Addison and Robert Youngblood. Wil was a sounding board for me as I started to see many of the sad departures that Christians have been making from biblical truth. He also helped me make the connection between the "gay Christian" movement and ways the social gospel is currently taking root in evangelicalism. Robert provided extensive notes on writing technique and clarity in an earlier draft, giving me confidence that my writing would be understandable as the manuscript neared completion.

This book would not have been possible without the generosity of Stephen Black and his team at First Stone Ministries in Oklahoma City. Stephen, Jim Farrington, Laura Leigh Stanlake, and Joseph Thiessen all gave of their time and ministry experience to help me understand the issues of homosexuality from both sides of the counseling couch. They are kind, Christ-exalting people who are a joy to spend time with. I am strengthened by the boldness of Stephen and the pastoral application of Jim. I didn't want to release this book without Stephen and Jim having read it first. Both men have become dear friends to me throughout this process.

I must also directly thank the following people:

Gareth Cockerill, who made sure I was properly understanding the biblical languages when I cited them.

Anthony Mathenia, who made sure I didn't reach beyond scripture in the book's bolder statements.

Justin Treadaway, Matthew Miller, Les Riley, Acey Floyd, Chuck Baggett, Jeremy Britt, Rob Bushway, and Andy Coburn, for being colaborers and brothers-in-arms. I have been sharpened through our friendship.

David H. Linden, who has not yet read anything I've written in this book but whose email correspondence on these topics has been humbling, invigorating, and insightful.

Steven Warhurst, who gave me hope with his statements at PCA General Assembly, while also exemplifying the simplicity of the work of faithful shepherding. It isn't about platforms and pithy statements but about diligence, perseverance, and consistency.

My pastor, Bill Bradford, who has let me vent and ramble to him throughout this process. His love of the truth and graciousness toward his flock helps me not lose heart.

My dad, Lyndon Perkins, who has lived out masculine integrity throughout my life and whose discernment and wisdom I hope to reflect as I age.

My wife, Betsy, whose relentless support and constant encouragement made sure I did not lose myself in despair. You are a gift more precious than riches.

And lastly, Robert Gagnon. I did not interact with him personally as I wrote this book, but it felt incomplete not to acknowledge how immensely beneficial his own book (and his other writing) is to anyone who wants to dig into the details on this subject. He is a gift to the people of God.

# RECOMMENDED RESOURCES

When writing a book on a topic as knotty and complex as homosexuality, it is inevitable that many aspects will be left unaddressed or only lightly covered. The following is by no means an exhaustive list of recommendations for further reading, but they are all books and websites that I have spent some time with and have found helpful.

## The Bible and the Church

*The Bible and Homosexual Practice: Texts and Hermeneutics*
Robert A. J. Gagnon (Abingdon Press, 2001)

This yet-to-be equaled volume is not for the casual reader, but anyone who wants to see every challenge to the biblical texts on homosexuality explained and debunked in highly detailed fashion need look no further. Gagnon's rigorous scholarship is intended to help defend the church from the onslaught of affirming scholarship. A go-to text for me in the writing of this book.

*Can You Be Gay and Christian? Responding with Love & Truth to Questions about Homosexuality*
Michael L. Brown (FrontLine/Charisma House Book Group, 2014)

Compassion and boldness mark this book, as Brown makes the case for why "gay" and "Christian" are incompatible identity markers for a child of God. As an able apologist, Brown answers pressing questions about biblical teaching while also being quite aware of the sociopolitical aspects of the LGBT movement and their influence on Christian thinking.

*The Gay Gospel? How Pro-Gay Advocates Misread the Bible*
Joe Dallas (Harvest House Publishers, 2007)

A wonderfully astute observer who writes from both conviction and personal experience, Dallas is able to talk about the elements of gay-affirming theology that can be enticing to a person in the pew while also showing where it is wrong, inconsistent, dangerous, and antibiblical. He is a warm-hearted evangelist who hopes that Christians will not simply know truth for its own sake but also be equipped for interpersonal conversations, denominational debates, and bearing public witness.

*The Grace of Shame: 7 Ways the Church Has Failed to Love Homosexuals*
Tim Bayly, Joseph Bayly, and Jürgen von Hagen (Warhorn Media, 2017)

Fearless in what they discuss and whom they implicate, the authors see the drift toward LGBT acceptance as not merely "out there" in liberal churches but also among conservative evangelical leaders and institutions. Some readers may wince at the authors' clear definitions of *masculine* and *feminine,* but I found this book immensely helpful in cutting through the clutter on these issues.

*What Does the Bible Really Teach about Homosexuality?*
Kevin DeYoung (Crossway, 2015)

A short, readable presentation of the biblical teaching on God's design in natural marriage and the sinfulness of homosexual behavior. If you need to get the gist of Gagnon's *The Bible and Homosexual Practice* without the deep technical writing, this is a good place to start. Sadly, Appendix 2 on "Same-Sex Attraction" creates more questions than it answers due to DeYoung's vague dealing with orientation and desire. Skip Appendix 2 and be helped.

## History and Society

*The Complete Guide to Understanding Homosexuality: A Biblical and Compassionate Response to Same-Sex Attraction*
Joe Dallas and Nancy Heche, general editors (Harvest House Publishers, 2010)

A collection of essays that succinctly cover the broad spectrum of topics related to homosexuality—from theology to medicine, counseling, parenting, and politics. Simply written and helpfully laid out, it is an essential resource for someone who needs a quick overview of homosexuality's impact in all those social arenas. Be aware that Alan Chambers and Randy Thomas have essays in the book; both have rejected the orthodox positions expressed here.

*Forgetting How to Blush: United Methodism's Compromise with the Sexual Revolution*
Karen Booth (Bristol House, Ltd., 2012)

Immensely important as both history and a case study in denominational drift. Booth details the influence of Alfred Kinsey's reports in the United Methodist Church in the 1960s, which led to greater compromises in the years ahead. Some of the revelations are quite shocking. I believe Booth makes too many accommodations for "gay celibate Christianity" in some spots, but her book is otherwise helpful.

*Love Thy Body: Answering Hard Questions about Life and Sexuality*
Nancy R. Pearcey (Baker Books, 2018)

Pearcey offers an insightful breakdown of the unspoken worldviews that have shaped our cultural views on abortion, hookup culture, homosexuality, and transgenderism—and discovers ways in which many Christians may have also been shaped by them.

*A Queer Thing Happened to America: And What a Long, Strange Trip It's Been*
Michael L. Brown (EqualTime Books, 2011)

An essential work that documents how the LGBT political agenda has consumed American society. Long and extensively footnoted, it offers a helpful play-by-play of LGBT victories in law, politics, education, entertainment, medicine, and the church.

*The Rise and Triumph of the Modern Self: Cultural Amnesia, Expressive Individualism, and the Road to Sexual Revolution*
Carl R. Trueman (Crossway, 2020)

A thoughtful untangling of the various philosophical threads that have led to the cultural chaos of the twenty-first century. If you want to understand how we got here as a society, Trueman's book is a must-read.

*Unnatural Affections: The Impuritan Ethic of Homosexuality and the Modern Church*
George Grant and Mark Horne (Legacy Press, 1991)

A short but helpful summary of the threats to biblical truth growing in society and in the church. The fact that it was written in the early 1990s makes it all the more prescient by giving much-needed context to our current day.

# Relationships and Pastoral Care

*Freedom Realized: Finding Freedom from Homosexuality & Living a Life Free from Labels*
Stephen H. Black (Redemption Press, 2017)

While sharing his own testimony of God's redemption in his life, Black also brings out many important insights from the closing of Exodus International—the large "ex-gay" ministry that has become the poster child of the supposed failure of orientation change. Black has decades of biblical counseling experience and offers many practical observations that will be helpful to the pastor, parent, or concerned Christian who wants to be better equipped for this discussion.

*The Homosexual Crisis in the Mainline Church: A Presbyterian Minister Speaks Out*
Jerry Kirk (Thomas Nelson, 1978)

How did a conservative evangelical write on this subject in 1978? Kirk proves to be a clear and compassionate voice, motivated by a deep love for the souls of people. Some of the detail regarding debates in his denomination will be of interest only to the twentieth-century church historian, but otherwise the book could benefit any reader.

*Pursuing Sexual Wholeness: How Jesus Heals the Homosexual*
Andrew Comiskey (Charisma House, 1996)

Writing with candid transparency and Spirit-worked humility, Comiskey not only presents his own story of struggle and transformation but also offers practical and biblically grounded guidance to those who desire to break free from homosexuality.

*When Homosexuality Hits Home: What to Do When a Loved One Says, "I'm Gay"*
Joe Dallas (Harvest House Publishers, 2015)

Gentle, empathetic, and honest in his presentation, Dallas writes to help Christian family members avoid spiritual compromise while preserving a relationship with a gay loved one. A really helpful book for anyone trying to navigate awkward and tense personal dynamics—especially parents and pastors.

# Online Resources

Stephen Black

www.stephenblack.org

Black is the executive director of First Stone Ministries. His website offers a number of helpful articles on political, pastoral, and theological topics and includes links to episodes of his podcast, *Freedom Realized LIVE.*

First Stone Ministries

www.firststone.org

Oklahoma City-based ministry dealing with same-sex attraction and other forms of sexual brokenness. Their website is full of helpful articles, recorded presentations, book recommendations, and personal testimonies of dozens of people who have found freedom from homosexuality and transgender identities. Biblically faithful and highly trust-worthy.

Robert Gagnon

www.robgagnon.net

Gagnon hosts links to PDFs of many of the articles he has written over the years on homosexuality and the Bible, including detailed critiques of specific secular and religious writings that have attempted to affirm homosexuality (from opinion editorials to book reviews). Whatever Gagnon writes on the subject is worth reading.

David H. Linden

www.davidhlinden.com

Includes many essays written by Linden. Most pertinent are his critiques of Side B/gay celibate theology within the Presbyterian Church in America (PCA). His writing may not seem immediately applicable to those in other denominations, but Linden clearly outlines exactly what makes the movement so unbiblical and dangerous.

*The New Atlantis*—Special Report on Sexuality and Gender (No. 50, Fall 2016)

Lawrence S. Mayer and Paul R. McHugh

https://www.thenewatlantis.com/issues/no-50-fall-2016

A special report released by two renowned psychiatrists on mental health issues related to homosexuality and gender dysphoria. Despite being a medical report, it was written for the general public—hoping to provide insight on the many common questions and misconceptions surrounding those issues. It counters many of the common claims put forward by LGBT activists. The entire report can be accessed online free of charge.

The Reisman Institute

https://www.thereismaninstitute.org/home

Over the last 40 years, Judith Reisman has been highlighting the impact of pornography and the sexual revolution on childhood development, education, and American society as a whole. Most notably, Reisman exposed the fraud and child abuse that undergirded Alfred Kinsey's sexuality studies in the 1940s. The Reisman Institute website is a compendium of links to dozens of articles, interviews, and books written by Reisman or about her work.

Warhorn Media
www.warhornmedia.com

Sharp and uncompromising, Tim Bayly and the rest of the Warhorn team provide insightful commentary on and analysis of the shifts and blurry language of contemporary evangelical leaders. Bayly's emphasis on repentance and biblical consistency is crucial in this current age of self-justification.

## More from American Family Association

*A Little Leaven: Confronting the Ideology of the Revoice Movement* (website/paper, 2021)
afa.net/alittleleaven

A paper I wrote for anyone who needs a more in-depth analysis of gay celibate theology and its challenge to orthodox theology. The PDF is free to download.

*AFA Cultural Institute: M.D. Perkins—Understanding the Dangers of "Gay Christianity"* (DVD, 2021)

A lecture where I present an overview of the three streams of "gay Christianity" and give some immediate applications for Christians. It can serve as an accessible introduction to the topic and why it matters.

*AFA Cultural Institute: Robert Gagnon—The Bible and Homo-
sexuality, Vol. 1 and Vol. 2* (DVD, 2016)

Video recordings of two talks given by Dr. Robert
Gagnon that examine the foundational issues in the debate
surrounding homosexuality in the church. Volume 1 focuses
on the proper interpretation of scripture, and Volume 2
focuses on the way God's design in creation should establish
our understanding of biblical sexual ethics.

*In His Image: Delighting in God's Plan for Gender and Sexuality*
(DVD, digital streaming, 2020)
www.inhisimage.movie

A feature-length documentary that seeks to answer culturally controversial questions about gender and sexuality
from a biblical perspective. Holding compassion and
conviction in equal measure, the film is intended to help
Christians understand the facts and be equipped to provide
care, counsel, and public witness on these crucial topics.

*The God Who Speaks: Tracing the Evidence for Biblical Authority*
(DVD, 2018)
www.thegodwhospeaks.org

A feature-length documentary that traces the evidence
of the Bible's authority through interviews with some of the
world's most respected biblical scholars. The film answers
common objections about the Bible's reliability and equips
believers to confidently base their lives on the power of
God's Word.

# SUBJECT INDEX

# SCRIPTURE INDEX

241